YOU DON'T WANT TO KNOW

Also by James Felton

52 Times Britain was a Bellend

Sunburn

JAMES FELTON

YOU DON'T WANT TO KNOW

SPHERE

SPHERE

First published in Great Britain in 2021 by Sphere

1 3 5 7 9 10 8 6 4 2

Copyright © James Felton 2021
Illustrator © Emanuel Santos 2021

A CIP catalogue record for this book is available from the British Library.

ISBN 978-0-7515-8080-8

Typeset in Caslon by M Rules
Printed and bound in Great Britain by Clays Ltd, Elcograf S.p.A.

Papers used by Sphere are from well-managed forests
and other responsible sources.

Sphere
An imprint of
Little, Brown Book Group
Carmelite House
50 Victoria Embankment
London EC4Y 0DZ

An Hachette UK Company
www.hachette.co.uk

www.littlebrown.co.uk

For Katie, Hugo and Dylan

INTRO

In what might be the shittiest marketing move of all time, I've decided to write a book detailing a bunch of events you specifically don't want to know about.

Why? Well, other than the honest answer above (shit at marketing), I'm hoping there are enough wrong 'uns in the world who are morbidly curious to read about topics such as: 'for ten years the Swedish thought Russia was invading their territory with submarines but it turned out to be herring farts'; or: 'there's a good chance you've made out with a woman who drowned over 100 years ago', and think 'Yeah, OK, I need to know a bit more about this.' Considering you've picked up this book and are now reading this sentence, I was clearly right to believe that such perverts exist. (If there's one thing I do know, it's my audience.)

There will be tales from science, medicine, history, incredibly recent history, and wherever weird facts lurk. To help ease down the grotesque information, I'll be making jokes the whole way through, like an inappropriate vicar at a funeral cracking gags about your gran.

So wherever you are – be it on a bus, a train, or curled up on your favourite toilet – sit back, relax and yet somehow brace yourself as you take in 75 tales about things you really don't want to know.

THE EXPLODING WHALE OF OREGON

In November 1970, an eight-ton sperm whale beached itself just off the Oregon coast. As far as send-offs go, blobbing your way onto a beach isn't the most dignified of affairs. For instance, if it happened to your nan you wouldn't say 'You know, this is just what she would have wanted.' But things were about to get a lot worse for the old whale, as is usual when several tonnes of dynamite gets introduced into a funeral.

The corpses of whales, due to some quirk of US law, fell at the time under the jurisdiction of the highway division. If you ever come across a whale carcass I'm sure you'll note how similar the problem of getting rid of it is to telling a driver to fix their tail lights, please, or doing some racial profiling.

In their wisdom, and following a call with the navy (who are world-renowned for solving their problems by blowing the shit out of them), the highway division decided to solve the whale problem by blowing the shit out of it. The plan was to get a big pile of dynamite and obliterate part of the whale, while firing the rest into the sea. The theory was that the dynamite would blow the bulk of the carcass far enough that it would drift into the ocean, leaving any smaller, more digestible (and let's face it, cooked) bits of delicious whale corpse scattered around the beach for smaller animals like seagulls to guzzle.

So far, so grim, but hardly anything to write home about. People blow up whales all the time in America, probably.

Now you'd think if you were going to bomb a whale to smithereens in front of the press (because of course they turned up), you'd sit down and have a bit of a think about how much dynamite you'd need, rather than just sticking twenty crates underneath it and saying 'That'll do.' Or maybe you'd at least listen to somebody with explosives training when they told you, 'I think you've overdone the old dynamite if I'm honest.' Well, you'd be wrong, and you're embarrassing yourself, quite frankly. Grow up.

Enter businessman and explosives guy Walt Umenhofer. He was on a drive around Florence, Oregon in a brand-new car he'd bought a few days earlier from a car dealership offering a 'whale of a deal' promotion (yes, really) when he happened upon the scene. Umenhofer had received explosives training during World War II and was not convinced the highway division – being, as you will soon discover, fucking idiots – had their calculations right.[1] He told them they either needed a lot fewer explosives to gently push it out to sea – he suggested twenty sticks, where they were using twenty crates – or a hell of a lot *more* to completely obliterate the carcass into tiny, chewable endangered whale nuggets for the birds.

The head of the project dismissed his advice, and Walt retreated as far as he could to watch the inevitable disaster. He went up to the road where his shiny new car was minding its own business and being generally whale free – which, to be fair, he should have found ominous. Joining him, alongside the local journalists documenting the whole debacle, were citizens who just fancied a bit of a gawp. Look, I'm a vegetarian, and I'm not saying I'm proud of myself, but if someone told me, 'There's a bunch of people at the beach who have never blown up a whale before and they're going to try and blow up a whale,' I'm not *not* pushing my way to the front.

All that was left to do before the grim spectacle unfolded was for project manager George Thornton to tell reporters – and this is a direct quote – 'Well, I'm confident that it'll work, the only thing is we're not sure how much explosives it'll take to disintegrate this thing.' At this point, I'm going to take this book multi-platform and beg you to go to YouTube, because there's a video.

4

You back? Good. If you didn't do as I recommended (why do I bother?), the explosion caused massive pieces of blubber to rain down from the sky onto buildings, cars in parking lots, and unsuspecting people who had previously been minding their own business and enjoying being whale-blubber free.

'Explosions in the movies usually look like a blast of fire and smoke,' one journalist in attendance that day, Paul Linnman, later said about the incident. 'This one more resembled a mighty burst of tomato juice.'[2]

The whale debris travelled so far that it hit Walt Umenhofer's new car, completely caving in its roof – the very same car that you'll remember from a few paragraphs ago he'd bought in a whaley good deal. 'My insurance company's never going to believe this,' Umenhofer reportedly said as a highway worker removed the blubber from his car with a shovel.[3]

After all this, the project manager told reporters that 'It went just exactly right.' Which is true, except of course that it's not.

THE WAR OF THE
HERRING FARTS

In the 1980s, a major diplomatic incident between nuclear super-powers could have been triggered by some farts that came out of the anus of a fish. In fact, Russia and Sweden nearly came to blows (yes, that's a fart joke) over fish farts, though neither of them knew it until long after the event. But before we move on to farts (patience, you deviant), some background.

In 1981, a Soviet submarine ran aground on the south coast of Sweden, just 6.2 miles from a Swedish naval base, beaching itself like a whale you really don't want to explode. The Soviets claimed that they were forced into Swedish territory by severe distress exacerbated by navigation errors – an excuse so bad they may as well have rummaged around in their backpack saying 'I'm sure my map's in here somewhere.' Sweden saw this as proof that the then Soviet Union was pissing around in Swedish waters, in the same way that a child will insist they aren't going to *eat* the cake, they just want to *hold* the cake. It didn't help calm things down at all when Swedish officials secretly measured for radioactive materials and detected what they were 90 per cent sure was a shitload of uranium-23 inside the sub, indicating that it might be nuclear armed. I should clarify at this point that this was a real submarine, not a fart.

It didn't look great. The submarine, despite supposedly being in distress, had navigated its way through some pretty ropey waters and rocks to reach the base.[4] As far as excuses go, 'I was just going for a bit of a ramble in the country' stretches your credulity if you notice the rambler's carrying a massive bomb right into MI6 HQ.

After interrogating the captain for a bit, the Swedish returned the submarine to international waters by tugboat. No record survives of the awkward 'So, any holidays planned, or are you too busy thinking of nuking the shit out of us?' chit-chat that took place in the cab while the sub was being towed.

The Swedish government remained on edge following the incident, convinced that Russian subs could still be operating near their territory. Right on cue, they began to pick up elusive underwater signals and sounds that seemingly confirmed their suspicions. In 1982, several of Sweden's subs, boats and helicopters pursued one of these unidentified sources for a whole month, only to find nothing.[5] Whatever technology these subs were using, they were tricksy, and appeared to disappear like a fart in a bath.

This carried on for well over a decade. Every time they picked up an acoustic signal, they would search and find nothing but a few bubbles on the sea's surface, in operations whose costs ran into millions of pounds, or whatever it is that Sweden used back then.

Sweden was worried about the intrusions, and couldn't think why, with the Cold War now over, the Russians would continue to provoke them in this manner, like a man two days after a badminton match that never happened hiding outside your house waggling around a big knife.

But Russia wasn't trying to provoke them at all. It was farts.

In 1996, Magnus Wahlberg, a professor at the University of

Southern Denmark, became involved in the investigation of the strange signals, to try and figure out how the submarines were so elusive. 'We were brought into this very secret room under the naval base of Bergen in Stockholm,' he explained in a TEDx Talk in 2012.[6] 'We were sitting there with all these officers and they were actually playing these sounds for us. It was the first time any civilian heard the sound.'

He had been imagining it to sound like the ping you hear in films when a submarine is detected, or just the noise of a propeller. 'It was nothing at all like that,' Wahlberg said in his talk. 'It sounded like someone frying bacon. Like small air bubbles releasing underwater.' He and a colleague headed home and put their heads together to figure out what could be making bubbles on a scale that would make Sweden think it was dealing with a potential nuclear war.

'It turns out herring have a swim bladder, and this swim bladder is connected to the anal duct of the fish,' Wahlberg said. 'It's a very unique connection, only found in herring. So a herring can squeeze its swim bladder, and that way it can blurt out a small number of bubbles through the anal opening.'

In layman's terms, they let one loose. Herrings swim in gigantic schools that can reach several square kilometres and up to 20 metres deep. When something gets near them – say, a hungry school of mackerel or a big fucking submarine on the lookout for Russian spies – it can frighten them, causing them to generate a lot of ass farts. The theory was that the Swedish government were roaming around the ocean looking for Russian submarines, scaring the shit out of the fish and then chasing the bubbles. They were trapped in a fish fart loop.

To test his hypothesis, Wahlberg bought a herring from a

8

shop and applied pressure to the sort of area you'd expect to make a fish fart, and sure enough, it made a sound that was at once very amusing and also confirmation of a scientific theory, like if Archimedes had farted the word 'Eureka'. He took footage of his test to the navy and played it back to them in the secret war room. It was a perfect match for the noise they had been hearing.

The good news was that Sweden wasn't under threat from Russia; the bad news was it had spent ten years deploying its fucking **military** in pursuit of fish farts. They thought they had been living under nuclear threat, but they had merely embarrassed some gassy fish, chasing them down after they let one out.

Since they figured out what was and wasn't fish farts, there have been zero reports of hostile intruders in Swedish waters. Thus ends the story of Das Toot.

WHEN PUSH COMES TO SHOVE, YOUR CAT WILL DEFINITELY EAT YOU

Y ou should probably know that your cat, though s/he refuses to eat the delicious premium cat food you buy it,
will happily chow down on your corpse the second you
don't have a pulse.

'Yes, your pets will eat you when you die, and perhaps a bit
sooner than is comfortable,' forensic anthropologist Carolyn
Rando told Buzzfeed News in a 2015 story on animals eating their
owners,[7] implying that these jerks aren't even *that* hungry. 'They
tend to go for the neck, face, and any exposed areas first, and
then, if not discovered in time, they may proceed to eat the rest
of you.' In one particularly horrible case she mentioned, a man's
body was found days after he had died, in 1994. His head, neck
and part of his arm had been defleshed 'right down to the bone'.[8]
Nearby, his ten cats, who had evidently treated him like a buffet,
also lay dead. The police figured out he had died of a prescription
overdose, which had also poisoned his pets when they consumed
his decaying corpse.

We're going to take a detour and talk about body farms now.
For those of you only interested in cats eating corpses, feel free to
think about them chomping away on Grandma for the next two
paragraphs.

Body farms are places where forensic scientists investigate the
decomposition of corpses, largely to help with criminal investigations. The idea is fairly simple: you take a bunch of corpses and
put them in a situation that will affect their decomposition which
you'd like to study, be it leaving them out in the open to rot or
inside the boot of a Ford Mondeo – which, due to their ample
boot space, are the go-to choice of car for knife-wielding maniacs.
You then sit there watching the corpse decompose and study the
results. Before these 'farms' existed, the law really had no idea of

the basics, such as how long it takes somebody to rot or how the process differs when they are underwater.

They're a surprisingly late invention, having not sprung up till the 1980s. Police thought they'd found a recently murdered body because American anthropologist William M. Bass mistakenly ruled that the corpse in question had died two to six months before. Actually the corpse was that of a Confederate Civil War officer whose body had been amazingly well preserved due to his cast-iron casket and very neat embalming. Bass realised that humanity, through not really being in the habit of staring at corpses for months on end, basically had shit-all idea of how bodies decomposed. And so he set up the world's first body farm in order to do just that. It's a testament to how good his idea and reputation was that when he pitched 'I want to watch people rot', security wasn't called immediately, and the idea went ahead in 1981.

Enter cats, looking hungry.

Body farms are generally outdoor areas, fenced off from ramblers with razor wire, or at least indicated by a big sign informing you it's not a nice place to hang around if you're already dead. Occasionally body farms will study the effects of scavengers on the bodies. And sometimes they won't, but scavengers will get in anyway.

In a particularly grim case study in 2020, two cats were seen breaking into the Forensic Investigation Research Station in Whitewater, Colorado.[9] The first cat ambled into the farm before feasting on a 79-year-old woman, going for anything soft and fatty. It returned night after night to feast on the woman, ignoring other corpses to finish its meal, over the course of thirty-five days. The second cat did the same, though targeting a 70-year-old man. The cat then left the man alone for a month before returning to eat some more, as though it was waiting for the man's flesh to age like a side of beef.

'What appeared to be the same cat was seen [on the camera traps] throughout the facility but showed no interest in any of the other 40-plus adjacent donors,' the researchers wrote in the study, in particularly horrifying detail. 'The cat did not scavenge new donors placed around the time of scavenging and in a similar stage of decomposition.'

Cats seem to show a preference for corpses in a state of decay. If they were just eating out of desperation I'd understand, but I draw the line at them being fussy. Next time somebody asks you whether you prefer dogs or cats, feel free to mention that dogs, though they require more walks, at least won't think of leaving your corpse for a few months to really bring out the flavour.

CHAINSAWS WERE ORIGINALLY INVENTED FOR CHILDBIRTH

Before the Caesarean section was widespread (or – oh sweet Jesus – anaesthetics), babies still had to find their way out of their mothers in emergencies. Even the really tricksy ones who looked at what was going on in the world at the time and decided 'Thanks but no thanks, wake me up when you've invented sanitation at the very least.' Caesareans have been around for millennia, but in the 1700s weren't particularly satisfactory if you'd planned on starting motherhood by not being dead.[10]

Well into the mid-nineteenth century, surgery involved so much cross-infection that Victorian episodes of *House* were ruined by every conclusion being the same: 'you got that dead guy's blood and accidentally put it in that guy and then he fucking died'. Surgeons operated while wearing coats which had been stiffened by the blood of previous patients. Not the most reassuring thing when someone comes in to operate on you and their manoeuvrability is clearly being compromised by the blood they evidently failed to keep on the insidey bits of someone else. Amongst surgeons, doing something like washing the blood of the dead off your coat was seen as being a bit prissy.

Where Caesareans were successful – and records are sketchy –

it was more likely to be out in the country, where operations took place with clean(er) equipment and on tables that hadn't been used for other surgeries. Basically, far away from maniacs who didn't think it was necessary to wash knives even after their thousandth unsuccessful surgery on a gangrene patient. Instead, you'd be performed on by the kind of maniac who would give complex surgery a crack with a kitchen knife, because at least the table was clean.

If you wanted to keep the mother alive, your options were somewhat limited. For a long time, doctors would increase the pelvic diameter by dividing the cartilaginous muscle connecting the left and right side of your pelvis. While the woman was still conscious, the surgeons would whittle away with a knife and then throw away the spare bits like they were a burger wrapper or an old battery or a third example of something that isn't a part of your actual crotch. This procedure was somewhat deceptively called a 'symphysiotomy'. I say deceptively because if someone tells you they're going to perform a symphysiotomy you probably picture the baby being lured out with a lute, rather than having your bone chipped away like a particularly busy waiter shaving down parmesan.

This system was both extremely painful and, oh god, messy, but worse was to come.

In the early 1780s, doctors John Aitken and James Jeffray put together a small chainsaw, powered by a hand crank like you'd see on a fishing rod. Now, instead of a painful procedure where your surgeon would cut at you with a knife, you'd look and see the reassuring sight of a surgeon spinning his hand around and around like he was sharpening a pencil down there. This hand-cranked nightmare tool was used throughout most of the nineteenth century. It wasn't until after numerous women had gone through this harrowing ordeal that people thought, 'Huh, this bad boy might be better suited to trees.'[11]

The worst part is, surgeons using a rudimentary chainsaw on your vagina was actually a vast improvement on what had taken place before. When you feel low about how the world is at the moment, remember you could be living through a time when strapping you down and grinding away on your crotch with a hand-cranked chainsaw was a step in the right direction.

CORPSES ARE USED AS ROAD SIGNS ON EVEREST

There's nothing more reassuring when going for a stroll than seeing the path littered with the dead who went before you. I imagine, I'm not much of a rambler.

Now picture climbing up the most treacherous mountain you'll ever be able to tackle here on Earth and having to pass by piles of people who – just like you – thought they'd have a crack at it, perfectly preserved in the ice with their optimistic smiles fixed on their face and maybe even doing a thumbs up. Now imagine that, occasionally, they're butt naked.

There are over 200 dead bodies on Everest. Recovering the bodies is expensive, at around $40,000–80,000 a pop. With no one willing to foot the bill, they are left up there, scattered around like the least appetising Calippo you'll ever see.

Some of the bodies are now used as landmarks by other climbers. For example, you'll know you're near the summit if you see the green boots of a climber who died under an overhanging rock on his way to the top in 1996. The boots are still on his feet. Even worse, in 2006, English climber David Sharp came across Green Boots during his descent from the summit (just as an aside, imagine thinking you're going to achieve the impossible and climb Everest, only to be named after the footwear on your corpse).[12] Sharp climbed into Green Boots' cave to rest his body (I'm guessing it doesn't rest your mind too much when you're near the top of a mountain and hanging out with a corpse in the dark), but, with his supplementary oxygen running out on one of the coldest nights of the year, things were not going well.

You probably picture Everest as an isolated place where you're alone for thousands of miles, but it's recently picked up more of a rush-hour-on-the-M5 vibe. While Sharp was huddled in the cave needing to be rescued, over forty climbers passed him from several different expeditions, all of whom assumed he was dead. It's that common a sight on Everest that even experienced leaders didn't blink or remark, 'Oh look, a fresh one.' He was eventually spotted by the leader of a Turkish expedition who, on the way up, believed Sharp to be newly dead, but on the way down noticed he was still breathing and moaning. Several teams attempted to rescue him after that, but – how can I put this delicately – Green Boots made a permanent friend.

If you've been waiting for the last three paragraphs for me to explain why some of the dead have their various genitals on display you should be ashamed of yourself, but here we go. These aren't people who were trying to join a more challenging version of the Mile High Club, nor victims of fresher hazing that got out of hand. The hikers appear to have reached a point where they were about to freeze to death and decided to take off their clothes and walk out into the snow, a phenomenon known as 'paradoxical undressing'. In around 25–50 per cent of deaths from hypothermia, in the final stages the victim will become confused, disorientated, hostile ... and naked. They take their clothes off, either due to damage to the hypothalamus (the area of the brain that regulates temperature) or because the muscles contracting the blood vessels in their limbs become so exhausted they relax, sending blood to the extremities, making the sufferer believe they're actually boiling hot. This is when they generally take their clothes off, usually starting with the trousers.

Victims who experience this often go further and start exhibiting 'terminal burrowing' behaviour, in other words they try to hibernate like a badger in any small space they can find. Acting this way is believed to be caused by an autonomous process of the brain stem. Away from Everest, this is often why a corpse found in a similar naked-burrowing situation is thought to have been murdered, because it's not often you see a naked dead body that's hidden itself in a trash compactor and think 'natural causes, that'.

Back to the naked dead on the mountain: if your relatives can't afford to recover your body, the closest thing to dignity for you is if other hikers take pity on you and throw you off the main trail down from the mountain, or cover your face so you're not staring out at everybody who walks past. Until, that is, climate change defrosts you like Jack Nicholson in *The Shining*, or an abandoned choc ice at the bottom of the freezer.

TRIAL BY GETTING WANKED OFF BY STRANGERS

In medieval times, if you married someone and then found out they were an insufferable jerk on a par with Piers Morgan, there weren't many routes to divorce. You were stuck with him for evermore, until one of you put the effort in and finally fucking died.

There was, however, one way to get your marriage dissolved, and it was a doozy. For at the time, there was no bigger crime for a married couple than not banging. The Lord, who got quite annoyed if you went to pound town before the marriage office, was absolutely flabbergasted if after getting married you refused to really plough each other. The law in parts of Europe agreed, and so intercourse with your spouse wasn't just encouraged, it was mandatory. If your husband was impotent, you could end the marriage.

Proving impotence to a court was even more humiliating than you're picturing in your sick, depraved mind. In England, sometime between December 1433 and February 1434, one William Barton went about proving he could get a boner.[13] He was stripped down and had his dong inspected by physicians, lawyers and a bunch of other random men and women who were up for it (and had been asked to come in as witnesses, sort of like how a blood spatter analyst may be called in for a trial today, but for stiffies).

About a dozen women and men testified that he did indeed have a magnum chopper, stating that he 'appeared sufficient to serve and to please any honest woman' and that it was larger than many of the men's own penises, which must be pleasing to have as a matter of legal record. However, the trials weren't over. As part of the legal proceedings, he was also about to get wanked off. 'The women made the same William remove his clothes down to his vest' – sexy – '[and] with cold hands they touched his yard' – I told you it was big – 'which because of coldness and the women's excessive and rough touching, and yet still on account of embarrassment, the said yard withdrew into his body.' Like a shy tortoise.

In the 1440s, John Skathelok was subject to the same test, with several women also showing him their breasts and genitals while giving him medieval dirty talk, of which there sadly is no record, but was probably along the lines of 'Hark! Thou art most pleasingly engorged!' That technique failed, and they instead turned to mocking him for not getting an erection.

In France, up until the revolution, things were even wilder and you could go through a 'trial by congress', where you would show a big room full of witnesses that you could, in fact, do a fuck.

Men who had had their marriage dissolved due to impotency, particularly amongst the richer aristocracy who could afford it, were willing to pay the hefty lawyers' fees involved to prove that they were potent. This wasn't to win the wife back like a teddy bear at the 'do a fuck, get a wife plush toy' stand at the fair, but more to show society that everything was just fine in your pants. As in medieval England, during the trials, the man would be prodded and poked to check whether he could get a hard-on on cue and come on command.[14]

'The experts waited around a fire,' one account of a trial in

22

Rheims read. 'Many a time did he call out: "Come! Come now!" but it was always a false alarm. The wife laughed and told them: "Do not hurry so, for I know him well." The experts said after that never had they laughed as much nor slept as little as on that night.'

In one particularly high-profile trial in 1659, Marquis de Langey was accused of being impotent and demanded to have the right to prove he wasn't. In front of a jury of fifteen people including matrons, surgeons and physicians, he attempted unsuccessfully to have sex with his ex-wife, finally giving up after two hours despite the clearly very romantic feel to the proceedings. He was mocked throughout France for this, despite not actually being impotent. He went on to have a second wife, and seven children.

I'm not saying the test is inaccurate, but if I wanted to get a divorce, even if we'd had loads of sex I'd fancy my chances that my husband wouldn't get a big old boner in front of a group of court-appointed strangers staring at his penis going, 'He sure looks impotent to me, this looks like a man who *cannot* for the life of him get an erection.'

PEOPLE WAKE UP DURING OPERATIONS. A LOT

You'd hope that your surgeons know more about general anaesthetics than 'if we put this gas in you, you go bye bye', but for centuries that pretty much *was* all they knew. We assumed that it somehow reduced communication between your brain cells, but if you pressed your surgeon for more information, they'd have told you 'Haven't got a fucking clue,' right before they gassed you.

Eventually we figured out that certain anaesthetics (we still don't know how the vast majority of them work) weaken the transmission of electrical signals between neurons in the synapses. We learned that in 2020. Apart from not having a fucking clue *how* they work, we're also not exactly perfect at using them. For the most part, it's pretty simple – you gas someone and they're knocked unconscious, then the surgeon plays around with their insides for a bit until they're either fixed or dead.

But for an unlucky cohort, the anaesthetic doesn't work as well as was intended, usually because the wrong dose is given. In these situations, you can be conscious during your own surgery. In some cases, you may be able to make the anaesthetist aware that something's not right, by moving an arm perhaps or flipping them off. It's made oh so much worse if you've been given neuromuscular blockers to keep you still during an operation, so that you can't actually move. In these situations you really are relying on one of the medical staff looking over and noticing: 'Oh look, Janet's eyes are screaming.'

Take, for instance, Carol Weihrer. Carol had been living with a chronic condition in one of her eyes for years, at which point she was advised to go for an ocular enucleation. That's medical speak for 'we're going to scoop your eyeball out with a spoon'. There's a reason why they use medical jargon, and I imagine it's because it's a lot more reassuring than a doctor smiling at you with a melon-baller saying 'Scoopy scoopy.'

She went in for prep, and was given her general anaesthetic and sweet, sweet paralysing neuromuscular blockers. Out went the lights. In what felt like seconds later, she came around and, seeing the lights of the hospital, assumed her operation was complete. However, this was one of those few instances when it feels like seconds have passed because that's literally how much time has passed. The operation hadn't started yet, but Jesus Christ was it about to.

She heard the relaxing music that was being played, the team discussing a problem with the ventilator, and worse, explaining to an intern everything that was going on. She tried with all her might to scream, but the paralysing drugs, the do-goody bastards, had done their job to a tee.

'I was lying there thinking, I can't survive this,' she told the *Guardian*.[15] 'Then I felt this tremendous tugging. I could only see this blinding light. The surgeon was saying, "Don't be afraid to use all the force you need. You really have to pull!"' She felt absolutely everything as her eyeball was scooped out like some particularly stubborn gelato and her vision went black.

Carol was one of the unlucky 0.1–0.2 per cent of patients, which may sound like nothing, but when you consider that, according to World Health Organization estimates,[16] 232 million surgeries are carried out annually, that's four hundred and eighty-four thousand people trying to tell surgeons with their eyes to put the scalpel down, or at least experiencing something that would haunt them for the rest of their lives, if the amnesia effect of the anaesthetic didn't do its job.

CARRY ON PENGUINS

In 1910, surgeon and zoologist George Murray Levick joined the Terra Nova expedition to the Antarctic, led by Robert Falcon Scott. While Scott was lucky enough to die on the trip, Levick was cursed to live on knowing precisely how horny penguins are.

Levick spent the summer of 1911–12 at Cape Adare, north-east Antarctica, smack bang in the middle of an Adélie penguin colony. This was an exciting opportunity for a scientist to observe the penguins' behaviour and win plaudits for describing it – or, just on a human level, to say whatever the repressed Edwardian equivalent was of 'Ooh, look at the lickle penguins'. Probably 'Hark, walky bird!' Unfortunately, he was unable to do either. As it turned out, this particular type of penguin was a nasty little pervert bird too disgusting to be documented in any science journal of the day.

Staying for an entire breeding cycle, Levick observed acts which were pretty vanilla by today's standards, yet would have made people at the time claw their own eyes out as recompense to God; as well as a bunch of acts so depraved that even David Attenborough would lose his knighthood were he ever to narrate them. As well as the usual stuff, like engaging in promiscuous sex with multiple partners, sex between two males, and wanking themselves against a rock (if you were Edwardian right now you'd be asking your butler for the fainting couch), he saw the cute little penguins participate in behaviour truly not befitting of any creature that's born wearing a tuxedo. We're talking rape, gang rape, necrophilia, necrophilia with females that had been dead for well over a year, and fatal sexual abuse of chicks in front of the parent birds. They never showed this in *Happy Feet*. They couldn't even be bothered to do it as a montage or a backdrop to a musical number for scientific accuracy.

Disgusted, Levick would only write about the penguins in Greek to keep the secrets away from those not educated enough to speak the language, or anyone who didn't happen to be Greek. Apparently they could learn about penguin necrophilia as much as they liked, Levick couldn't give a shit.

In one event that he found particularly harrowing, he watched as one female penguin, half dead, dragged herself across the rocks on her belly 'using her flippers for propulsion as her legs trailed uselessly behind her'. He was wondering whether to kill her out of mercy, when penguin after penguin ran up and 'without any hesitation, tried to mount her'.[17] An image so disturbing it isn't even lightened by imagining any of the participants as Pingu. A few days later, he came back to find the penguin even more bruised and battered from the birds, which he dubbed 'hooligans'. Which is a bit like calling Charles Manson or Jack the Ripper a bit of a rapscallion the day after their spree.

There's something quite heartbreaking about reading Levick's excitement at seeing the adorable birds up close, shortly before he was forced to write entries like:

> This afternoon I saw a most extraordinary sight. A Penguin was actually engaged in sodomy upon the body of a dead white-throated bird of its own species.

28

> The act occurred [for] a full minute, the position tak-
> en up by the cock differing in no respect from that
> of ordinary copulation, and the whole act was gone
> through down to the final depression of the cloaca.

In a subsequent experiment in 1974, a team of scientists tried to figure out what exactly the limits of these perverts were. D. G. Ainley and his team observed the Cape Crozier colony and found much of the same behaviour, so, naturally, they placed a frozen dead female in a nest to see what would happen. Of course the answer was that the other penguins either did a bit of necrophilia, or tried to shove it out of the nest. During the course of the experiment, the dead penguin became 'damaged by repeat deployments', a sentence whose import can only be made worse by the following sentence: 'it was found that just the frozen head of the penguin, with self-adhesive white "O's" for eye rings, propped upright on wire with a large rock for a body, was sufficient stimulus for males to copulate and deposit sperm on the rock.'

As Levick puts it, 'there seems to be no crime too low for these Penguins'.

THE WORLD TREATS NUCLEAR WEAPONS WITH THE SAME 'OFF YOU FUCK' ATTITUDE KIDS SHOW THEIR GLOVES

L ook, I'm going to level with you, I'm a forgetful person. If my wife asks me to pick up the kids there's a good chance I'll forget until the social workers show up two days later asking 'What the shit?' But if I was in charge of a device that could kill millions of people at once, I'd like to think I wouldn't lose it like some fucking keys.

People who don't think like this, it transpires, are the ones charged with keeping track of actual nuclear weapons. Since their invention in 1945, humanity has had thirty-two accidents with nuclear weapons. They refer to these events as 'Broken Arrows', which is quite a folksy way of saying 'we nearly fucking nuked the shit out of millions of people'. It's like calling a murder spree 'a bit of a stabby snafu'.

We've also completely lost six of them. I'll outline just a few of the accidents because, and I can't believe I'm saying this, there isn't enough room to talk about all the nuclear accidents we've had over the years.

The igloo
At Lakenheath Air Base in Suffolk, England, the US Air Force conducted a training exercise involving a B-47 bomber, which somehow managed to crash into a nuclear weapons storage facility known as an 'igloo'. The igloo contained Mark 6 nuclear weapons, three of which were knocked into by the bomber in what I'm imagining was probably the highest-stakes game of skittles ever. That was the least of their worries, however. The aircraft then exploded, showering burning fuel over the facility. The bomb disposal officer called it a 'miracle' that one of the Mark 6 bombs – which sound much more powerful than Mark 1 through 5 if my hobs are anything to go by – 'with exposed detonators' didn't explode.[18] Quite

why they conducted a training exercise next to a nuclear storage facility, like a clown holding fire-juggling auditions in an Esso forecourt, is unclear.

Do not pull the lever

In one of the most cartoonish incidents to involve a nuclear weapon, a US aircraft was due to carry nuclear bombs from the US to the UK as part of a mock bomb drop.[19] In other Broken Arrow incidents, we'd decided to use real nuclear bombs (sometimes armed, sometimes not) to give the pilot a feel for the weight of the device – because apparently we had mastered the technology to split the atom but hadn't quite figured out how to make a paperweight really big – but in this case, the plane was carrying real nuclear weapons just on the off chance that war with the Soviet Union broke out. Smart.

During the flight, navigator and bombardier Captain Bruce Kulka was summoned to the bomb bay area after an error light in the cockpit started flashing, showing a problem with the bomb harness locking pin. Kulka reached around the bomb to pull himself up, but grabbed the emergency release lever by mistake. Not bad for a guy whose main job is to be good at bombs and navigating.

The bomb fell on the doors below, smashing them open, before dropping another 15,000 feet and creating a 75ft-wide, 30ft-deep crater in the backyard of a family in Mars Bluff, Florence County, South Carolina, totally destroying their house and damaging several nearby homes. Luckily, the core of the missile was stored elsewhere on the aircraft and even the captain hadn't been clumsy enough to install it as he tried to fumble his way into the cockpit. To be fair to the bombardier, if you have a release lever right next to an entrance hatch for a nuclear weapon, maybe splash out a few dollars on a THIS IS NOT A BANISTER sticker.

Finding Bombo

Probably the most disconcerting Broken Arrow mishaps are the ones where the bombs were never found. Out there, at least six nuclear weapons are just lying around, waiting to be discovered by the people each of them will immediately kill within a 100-mile radius.

In one incident, a B-47 bomber straight up disappeared in March 1956. The plane was supposed to be refuelled over the Mediterranean Sea but didn't make contact over the radio, and was never seen or heard from again. Then in 1958, yet another B-47, this time carrying a Mark 15 bomb (in terms of gas hobs we're talking full boil), struck an F-86 aircraft during a 'simulated' combat training mission. After attempting to land, but finding their damaged plane too weighty, the crew decided to drop a nuclear bomb into the Savannah River. The bomb didn't detonate, and they managed to land. But the bomb is still missing and, this I really must stress, is a nuclear fucking bomb.

And finally, in December 1965, the US got cartoony again when an A-4E Skyhawk aircraft carrying a nuclear weapon rolled off the back of an aircraft carrier in the Philippine Sea near Japan. The plane and its pilot were never seen again, and the hydrogen bomb remains with them somewhere on the floor of the ocean near the Japanese island of Okinawa. It's feasible that pressure could one day crack the weapon's casing, which sounds bad. But at least we'll finally know its location when every marine animal within swimming distance is suddenly either dead or suspiciously green.[20]

A FRIENDLY GAME OF EEL YANK TURNED INTO A CITY-WIDE RIOT

In nineteenth-century Amsterdam, the residents used to enjoy a game of 'eel pulling', in which they'd tie a rope across a moat, canal or river and attach a live eel to the middle of it. Players – and I really do use that term loosely – would then get in boats and attempt to grab the slippery bastard without falling into the water, with the winner taking home the equivalent of about a week's wages. The game was eventually prohibited for being cruel, though I'm sure you could make an argument for it being banned on the grounds that it's the single most insane yet simultaneously dull sport you've ever heard of, excluding cricket.

On Sunday, 25 July 1886, however, people on the Jordaan in Amsterdam really, really fancied a wholesome game of 'eel pulling'. Fish sellers strung up a rope across the canal between house numbers 184 and 119 and soon residents were fighting to get an eel off the rope, probably while shouting 'Fuck the police'[21] across the canal.

Four policemen noticed the people in boats attempting to grab the eel, and decided to cut the rope to stop the festivities. Unfortunately for them, they hadn't banked on just how much the

34

players of 'yanking the eel off a rope in a boat' absolutely loved to yank that eel off a rope in a boat. It turned out that they were also big fans of the old ultra-violence.

The players and spectators threw one of the policemen into a basement and beat him mercilessly, while the other four fled to gather reinforcements.[22] Before you feel too sorry for the eel defenders, the police were massive fans of their own game: doing a police brutality. With both sides unable to keep things in proportion (you know how it is when you're in the heat of a game of eel yank) the fight evolved into a full-on riot. The more police officers, the bigger the crowd grew, the more police officers were called in. Kettles, pots, plants, roof tiles, paving stones and boulders were thrown at the police, before one group grabbed an inspector and beat the crap out of him and even discussed drowning him in the canal. (Look I don't endorse it, but I've got to question your judgement as a policeman if you're willing to fuck with people who torture eels for fun.) As luck would have it, they were talked out of it by one of the more sensible eel rioters. The first day of rioting was finally quelled at 10 p.m., presumably when the players realised it was way too late now to yank eel anyhow.

The next day, having slept on it, people were still shitting their teeth about how their game of eel had been broken up, and the crowds headed to the police station looking for a fight. This time it got so out of hand that the army was called out, and in the ensuing carnage twenty-five people were killed. Don't want to be a prick about it, but you never get this kind of death toll with badminton. Two thousand rioters were given prison sentences.

Like a passive-aggressive flatmate picking a fight about the washing up, it wasn't really about the eels. The disparity between the rich and poor in the city had grown enormous, so it was probably a lot to do with that. The eel game was their 'last pleasure', and they snapped when that was taken away from them. Which speaks volumes about how terrible conditions must have been, to be honest. I mean, how bleak does life have to become before your only solace is yanking an eel off a rope?

WE USED TO TRY AND REVIVE PEOPLE BY BLOWING TOBACCO SMOKE UP THEIR ARSEHOLES

It seems strange to think now, what with science and that song about what bone is connected to what other bone, but for the vast majority of human history medicine wasn't based on anything other than shoving stuff in various orifices and just sort of seeing what happened next.

Inevitably, this led to someone seeing a dead guy and thinking, 'Yeah, I might blow me some tobacco smoke up his arsehole, see if that makes him not dead.' The indigenous people of North America were the first to try the Forbidden Combo, and they even developed a traditional bum tube they'd breathe smoke through to stimulate breathing. When we Europeans went over there, we followed our time-honoured tradition of nicking stuff and decided to try the idea out on the dead folks back home.

It became a common 'cure' for people who drowned, and kits for blowing smoke were even placed along the River Thames, the way you'd expect to see lifebelts today except there's less chance of them going up your arse. The kits even came with a set of bellows, because the Brits are sophisticated types who, when attempting to introduce smoke into someone's arsehole, are above blowing it in there themselves and prefer to pump it in like we're blowing up a fucking lilo.

One particularly harrowing example of this method of 'resuscitation' involved a woman in 1650 – Anne Greene – who had been sentenced to death for infanticide, though it was likely she'd had a miscarriage. She was taken to be hanged at Oxford Castle on 14 December, where she asked for her friends to pull at her hanging body and a soldier to hit her with his musket in order to spare her pain and speed up death. After an hour, people – as you would – believed her to be dead and cut her down, before sending her to Oxford University for dissection.

The next day they opened up the coffin and found she had a pulse and was breathing. Apologies, I'll spare you the medical mumbo-jumbo: I mean it was time to start inserting a pipe into her anus.

Such was the advanced knowledge of Oxford physicians at the time that they immediately began bloodletting and trying to heat up her extremities. Which is like finding someone who's been in a traffic accident, stabbing them in the liver then wrapping them in a foil blanket. They proceeded to give her a 'heating odoriferous Clyster to be cast up in her body, to give heat and warmth to her bowels',[23] which is olde-timey medical talk for you jamming a single pan pipe up the old bumhole.

All's well that ends well – she actually survived and was pardoned, as they believed that God had saved her. Which must have been a bit of a kick in the teeth for the doctors who went to the trouble of sending old smokey to brown town.

A KING ONCE EXPLODED ONTO HIS FUNERAL PROCESSION

The human body is disgusting long before it's crawling with maggots and melting into juice. Having spent all your life trying to live in dignity, it's very upsetting that seconds after you die, your neurons stop functioning, meaning your brain stops secreting hormones to regulate bodily functions. Every muscle in your body relaxes and you enter primary flaccidity. *Every* muscle, if you catch my drift. No? Well, after you die, everyone catches *your* drift because without control of your sphincters you straightaway shit and piss yourself. OK, you've got bigger problems being dead, but it's pretty embarrassing that your final goodbyes are shortly followed by a brief moment of confusion when your relatives try to figure out if you've actually died or merely let one rip.

The indignity of death did, however, provide a fitting end for a king who was an absolute arsehole. William the Conqueror was originally known as William the Bastard, due to his parentage. After tapestrying his way into the history books by winning the Battle of Hastings with a cheeky arrow to King Harold (or mutilation, the tapestry is unclear. Side point, but I need to get this off my chest: tapestries, while fun to look at, make shit battle reports), the new ruler took on the name William the Conqueror. He then set upon doing murders that would fully justify his previous name of William the Bastard.

Well known for handing out limb-chopping punishments to criminals, his pièce de resistance was nevertheless the 'Harrying of the North',[24] in which he sent men to loot, slaughter and burn crops across vast swathes of the north of England in order to punish his enemies. He operated a scorched-earth policy, destroying crops and tools so that anyone left alive would likely starve to death, which was especially insulting to towns that are largely named after a food. In some areas of the north, over 70 per cent of the population died or else got the hell out of Dodge for ever, never to return. His act was regarded as particularly cruel, even back in the days when flaying was seen as a bit of a giggle.

Which is all to say you shouldn't feel bad about enjoying the events leading up to and following his death.

In 1077, William's sons Henry and William Rufus played a clever 'prank' on their brother Robert, pouring a full chamber pot – presumably full of shit and piss – over his head.[25] These were the early days of the prank, long before anyone would think of the much more sophisticated idea of doing exactly the same thing and recording it for YouTube. Robert started a fight with his brothers, which was eventually broken up by his dad. When his dad failed to punish his brothers adequately, Robert reacted the next day by attempting to seize the castle of Rouen. Oh come on, we've all lashed out after a squabble. This began years of on-off battles with his son, during which William sustained a fatal injury. William had been eating like a king for years, and, while launching a war against his own son in 1087, his horse reared up and pushed part of the saddle into his somewhat large abdomen, piercing his intestines.

After a number of days, he passed away. Normally, at this time, it was expected that the people who had attended to you in life would arrange your funeral. This was a problem for William, as the people who had attended to him in life fucked off the very moment he died, having not liked him very much at all. His body was left lying in a medical facility in Rouen, where his clothes were stolen and he remained, whiling away the hours by decomposing naked on a slab.

Eventually a passing knight volunteered for the duty of taking care of the corpse. He gave embalming the already partly decomposed cadaver a go, before taking the body seventy miles to Caen to be buried. The whole long, leisurely way, the king spent his days enjoying his new hobby of filling his various cavities with gas from decomposition.

When they eventually arrived at the Abbaye-aux-Hommes, a fire in the city warmed the corpse, further expanding the gases. An argument broke out with a local man, who claimed he owned the land on which William was to be buried; haggling ensued until the man was paid compensation, while William's bloated corpse became so large during that time that it would no longer fit into the stone sarcophagus that was to house him. Not to be deterred, the gravediggers attempted to cram him in there anyway, like trying to force a can of baked beans into an already full can of dog food. His 'swollen bowels burst, and an intolerable stench assailed the nostrils of the by-standers and the whole crowd'.[26]

The funeral continued, though quite a bit more hurriedly than was intended. You tend not to hang around for the wake when you're covered in king juice, in my experience.

SCIENTISTS BLINDED CATS TO TEST WHAT MAKES THEM LAND ON THEIR FEET

Science, to be fair to it, has answered a lot of questions, from 'Why apple fall down?' to 'How do we cure smallpox?' But it's also posed a lot of questions that didn't really need an answer. One study, for instance, looked at whether toast really does land butter-side down more often than not, and found that it did. Which is great, but I've just googled it and apparently cancer still exists. Cheers scientists, good to know why my floor is buttery, that's so much more important.

Then there are questions so trivial that they make the experiment unjustifiable. I'll cut to the chase: scientists once scooped out the eyeballs of cats in order to determine how they land on their feet.

Before the scientists got out their eye fork and set it to cats' eyes, it had already been documented that cats were able to right themselves as they fell, and that it had something to do with both their sight and the vestibular system in their ears, which gives them their sense of balance. Scientists also knew, thanks to another experiment, that if you blindfold an adult cat then throw it in the air like an angry football it will still right itself to an extent,

44

though blindfolded cats land a bit more awkwardly as they don't know how far they are off the ground.

I know you're thinking 'That's probably enough knowledge on how cats land,' but that's the mundane opinion of somebody who doesn't possess their own eye gouger with a cat setting. Scientists in France decided that the fairest way to find out more was to study cats who had had their eyes plopped out shortly after birth, before they'd had a chance to see that they'd arrived in cat hell, aka dog heaven.

They took six kittens that had been blinded within their first week after birth by enucleation – which, as discussed earlier, is a fancy way of saying popped out like you're removing an avocado pit with a spoon – and four that hadn't been blinded as a control. Then, for the next fifty days, the 'scientists' – a word that somehow stands in for 'cat torturers' in this instance, though only because they took the time to write a hypothesis – took the cats and dropped them spine first to the ground, four times a day until they reached maturity.

Also, maybe for science or maybe just to keep things spicy, the scientists began throwing the kittens up into the air to see how that would affect the results. As it turns out, in the early days it wasn't a lot. The problem for the kittens was that they were in fact kittens, and hadn't learned to right themselves yet. For the first twenty-five days, both the blinded cats and the lucky cats (here 'lucky' means 'thrown from heights a lot but while in possession of eyeballs') righted themselves about as much as each other, which is to say not at all. They would be dropped to the ground, twat themselves, then wait around for their next mid-morning twatting. Around the 25-day mark, the cats did begin to right themselves as they went down and from then on had a nice soft landing on their feet, but to say this in the defence of the scientists is like defending a criminal charged with repeated GBH on the grounds that the victim got used to the twattings.

The blinded cats righted themselves in the air, but weren't as good at the final landing part. From this, the scientists learned that cats' righting mechanism operates largely through their sense of balance, with vision playing a role in the landing.[27] The applications of which are fucking non-existent.

YOUR FAVOURITE CEREAL WAS DESIGNED TO STOP YOU WANKING

The man behind the company that created Rice Krispies, Frosted Flakes and Coco Pops was not a big fan of wanking, or of anybody who wasn't white.

John Harvey Kellogg was born in 1852 – a particularly prudish time in history, I'll grant you. It was a time when women would ride a horse side saddle because to ride a horse like a, well, horse, was considered too sexual.[28] Even by the standards of the day, Kellogg went well above the call of duty, and it's widely believed that he never consummated his marriage. He also wrote part of his book about why we should all stop nobbing while on his honeymoon, a time usually reserved for said nobbing.

In this 798-page book – he really, really didn't like people to boff – he begins the chapter on 'the solitary vice' by seriously hyping up wanking. 'Its frequent repetition fastens it upon the victim with a fascination almost irresistible', he wrote, later adding that there's an 'alarming prevalence of the vice', confirming it was all the rage in those days.[29] He goes on to quote medical authors of the era, saying 'neither the plague, nor war, nor small-pox, nor similar diseases, have produced results so disastrous to humanity as the pernicious habit of Onanism', which is hyperbole even if you are writing from the perspective of a teenager's sock drawer.

The book made specific claims about how the act harmed people, recounting symptoms such as mood swings, bad posture (I'm imagining slightly hunched) and acne, which is – in a weird coincidence – basically a diagnosis for being a teenager. He also believed it caused a fondness for spicy foods ('Sheila, I think Harold's been cranking it again, he keeps asking for jalfrezi') and that, in extreme cases, people could wank themselves to death, writing that 'such a victim literally dies by his own hand'. No, he did not clarify how you could crank your way into the next life, nor provide diagrams of the technique.

Kellogg thought that one of the ways to deal with this (and brace yourself for worse) was to give people plain, boring foods, thinking that meat and flavourful foods increased your urge to have sex. Who amongst us doesn't want to go to pound town when you're bloated from a massive Chinese takeaway? His cereals, including granola and Kellogg's Corn Flakes, were an attempt to make a cereal so boring it would stop you from jacking it, like a chastity belt you can chew. Thankfully his more business-savvy brother moved the business away from this sort of branding, and we never had to hear Tony the Tiger say, 'Theeeeeey're to stop you ejaculating.'

Surprise surprise, eating shit cereal doesn't really work in a way that'll make you stop touching yourself, other than for the brief period in which you are eating it. But Kellogg had another trick up his sleeve to stop people, and it was a bit of an escalation. It can be summarised as this:

'Right, eating cereal hasn't worked, time for some genital mutilation.'

Kellogg was the leader of an anti-masturbation movement, and he advocated circumcising boys in the most painful way possible as a means of keeping them from touching themselves. 'The operation should be performed by a surgeon without administering an anesthetic,' he wrote. 'As the brief pain attending the operation will have a salutary effect upon the mind, especially if it be connected with the idea of punishment, as it may well be in some cases.' He also favoured sewing the foreskin together with a single wire, to make it impossible to get an erection, tying the victims' hands together, and placing their genitals in his own patented penis cage. In girls, he preferred enemas, 'the application of blisters and other irritants to the sensitive parts of the sexual organs', applying carbolic acid to the clitoris, and, of course, the removal of the clitoris altogether.

It's a testament to how utterly bizarre his views on doing the five-dog dance were that people barely mention that he was massively into racial segregation and eugenics, including wanting to sterilise the mentally ill. Which was a bold move for someone going around talking about mutilating genitals and designing anti-wanking breakfast treats.

THE MAN WHO FOUGHT WORLD WAR II FOR THREE DECADES

Hiroo Onada was a soldier in the Japanese army who ended up fighting World War II for longer than anybody else on Earth. By the time he'd finished, flared jeans had come into and were beginning to go out of fashion.

Onada was a second lieutenant when he was given his biggest mission. As an intelligence officer, he was to go to Lubang Island in the Philippines. He was ordered to conduct guerrilla warfare on the island, to never give up, and not to die. Like the three laws of robotics that always end up getting Will Smith killed in *I, Robot*, there was a flaw in these orders that would become apparent in the next few decades.

When he arrived, he met up with fellow Japanese soldiers, but shortly thereafter the Americans arrived and overwhelmed them. Following his orders to the letter, Onada refused to die and was left there with three other soldiers, hiding out in the mountains like fucking Predator. Here he would remain for many years, emerging to conduct warfare, kill quite a few people, and steal food, which kind of paled in comparison to all the killing. I should point out here that he arrived on the island in February 1945, so the years of killing mainly took place in peacetime.

The first sign they were given that the war was over was in October 1945 when they found a leaflet informing them that the war was over. The group dismissed it, believing it to be Allied propaganda, and thinking that if the war was *really* over they wouldn't have been shot at by police when they conducted their own killings. During peacetime, police famously say merely, 'Crack on, lads, get some killing under your belt, son,' so you could see why they were confused.

At the end of 1945, leaflets were dropped by the Japanese in an attempt to tempt the soldiers out of hiding, including surrender orders signed by their superior General Tomoyuki Yamashita. It was at this point that Onada decided to become really pernickety about spelling. 'The leaflets they dropped were filled with mistakes so I judged it was a plot by the Americans,' he explained in an interview in 2010.[30]

One soldier, Yuichi Akatsu, walked away in September 1949 and surrendered to Philippine forces, just four short years after the war was over, demonstrating real commitment problems that I'm sure troubled his career from then on. The others decided to be even more cautious, in case Akatsu had given away their location. Ever more desperate to stop the remaining soldiers, the Japanese began dropping family photos to them as proof that they weren't being deceived, but Onada believed this too was one of their clever tricks. The gang of three became two when Shimada was killed in 1954 by a search party looking for the men. Then, a full twenty-eight years after the war was over, while burning down a rice harvest as part of their military activities, Onada's final companion was killed by police in 1972, the year a post-WWII (but still clearly deeply traumatised) world went tits over Donny Osmond's 'Puppy Love'.

Hiroo spent a further two years by himself before a Japanese explorer came and sought him out. When Norio Suzuki found Onada, he still wouldn't surrender, saying he would only take orders from his superior officer, shifting the goalposts once again. Upon his superior officer's arrival on the island he finally accepted he wasn't a brave soldier fulfilling his duties against all odds but merely a bog-standard serial killer with massive trust issues. He turned himself in to the police, but was pardoned by President Ferdinand Marcos on the grounds that he had only slaughtered a bunch of people because he thought he was still fighting a war. Which – little tip for you – apparently earns you around thirty freebies.

JIZZING OUT WORMS IN THE NAME OF SCIENCE

There have been quite a few cases of scientists successfully experimenting on themselves and everything going swimmingly, but for every genius injecting themselves with polio and finding the cure, there are at least ten people who *thought* they were geniuses and ended up giving themselves gonorrhoea, probably having to explain to their partners, 'Look, I haven't cheated, I'm just thick.' Here follow a few of my favourite self-experiments gone wrong.

Claude Barlow

Researcher Claude Barlow wanted to study parasitic flatworms called schistosomes. The worms are generally released from infected freshwater snails, and when they enter humans through the skin they cause horrible symptoms ranging from abdominal pain and diarrhoea to bleeding from the pee hole. Left untreated, they can cause infertility, organ damage and bladder cancer. As the worms were to be found in Egypt, Barlow tried to get them posted to the US. When that scheme failed (because they all died in their Jiffy bags), Barlow naturally decided to go to Egypt and transport them himself, by gulping down 200 of the critters. Which seems like a lot, and to be honest makes me think he just liked the taste.

He became desperately ill, but refused treatment as he wanted to keep the parasite inside himself until he had Deliveroo'd them home to the US, at which point he'd piss them out, to the applause of colleagues. Or so he thought. He ended up pissing out 200 eggs in his urine and ejaculating a further 4,630 eggs in his semen, which is incredibly upsetting even when you don't picture them as full-sized hen's eggs – NO, STOP, I SAID DON'T PICTURE IT! Once they were out, the US government, for whom he'd done the task, decided they didn't want to use his eggs. Which was a shame, as he was still full of them and their parasite parents.

It was eighteen months later and just after the war ended when he finally spunked them all out, which meant he couldn't even complain about his ordeal. Who wants to be the guy responding to somebody's harrowing war story with 'Hey, you'll never guess what I've just jizzed'?[31]

The guy that necked vomit for no reason

In the early nineteenth century, American doctor Stubbins Ffirth believed that yellow fever wasn't an infectious disease, and set out to prove it in the most disgusting manner imaginable.

First, he collected various fluids from infected patients. He then made a wound in his arm and poured in some vomit, before pouring more vomit into his eyeballs and then drinking it. After not being infected, he moved on to experimenting with patients' blood, saliva and piss.

Of course, it turned out yellow fever was an infectious disease. He didn't get ill, but only because he had collected his fluids from patients in the last stages of the disease, when it was no longer infectious. He had been necking puke and piss and rubbing it into his blood for absolutely no reason at all.[32]

John Hunter

There are two versions of this tale, which takes place in 1786, though I'm not sure which is worse. In one version, John Hunter injected himself with gonorrhoea,[33] wanting to prove that syphilis and gonorrhoea were caused by the same pathogen. If he got both, he figured, it would prove him correct. To his absolute delight he did contract both potentially fatal genital diseases, and concluded that he was right and also very, very itchy 'down there' [nods at penis]. Not only was he experiencing pain in the testicles, he was also completely wrong. The patient from whom he'd taken the samples to inject himself with had more venereal diseases than Rasputin's toilet seat, rendering Hunter's whole experiment invalid, though he didn't know it. The patient didn't just have gonorrhoea as Hunter assumed – he had gonorrhoea, syphilis and herpes. So Hunter ended up with all three, too.

Unfortunately, Hunter was left with two things: an incredible reputation and a burning sensation when he peed. When he published the conclusion that gonorrhoea caused both syphilis and gonorrhoea, medicine pretty much said 'OK, warty' and accepted it as fact. He set back investigations on the subject by about fifty years, causing even more damage to science than his own peen.

In the second version of the story, he did exactly the same experiment, but on some other human guinea pig, giving them the horrendous diseases for the same noble purpose of setting science back decades.

Charles Babbage

Everyone feels pretty idiotic every now and then. For instance, I once lost my phone on the train and googled 'Who do you report a lost phone to' on what turned out to be my phone. But whenever

I think to myself 'I'm dumb', I console myself with the knowledge that Charles Babbage – supposed genius and creator of the first mechanical computer – once baked himself in an oven at 130 degrees like a fucking pie just to see what would happen.[34]

The mathematician, engineer and baked potato, born in 1791, was obsessed with fire. The cooker incident, in which he placed himself in the oven for a full four minutes, was just a starting point. He later organised a trip for himself to Mount Vesuvius, before being lowered inside so that he could get close to the lava.

August Bier

August Bier was a party doctor, by which I mean he once injected cocaine into his own cerebrospinal fluid as a test, to see if it would be suitable as an anaesthetic. Well, I guess he's the biggest party animal you can be as a doctor while still getting your antics printed in a medical journal. The experiment on himself went wrong, and he sprung a spinal fluid leak. You don't need to be Dr Phil to know that leaking spine goo is not great. So, having proven that there were risks, he got his assistant Hildebrandt to have a go, and injected *him* with cocaine instead.

Once he established his faithful assistant was numb, he began absolutely twatting the guy, kicking his shins, inserting a pin down his femur, hitting said shins with an iron hammer, and plucking his pubic hairs (which I'd say is a bit of an HR no-no), before mashing his testicles with forceps.[35] The pair celebrated their success later that evening with cigars and wine, and by success I mean that time one of them smacked the ever-living shit out of the other's testicles and shins with no horrendous pain until the very second the anaesthetic wore off.

MOBY-DICK WAS BASED ON A COMPLETE HORROR STORY

Moby-Dick is the best story out there about a protagonist who, after getting injured by an animal, decides to dedicate the rest of their lives to pounding the crap out of it.

Part of *Moby-Dick* was based on the tale of the *Essex* whaleship, which in 1820 ran into a series of unfortunate events that makes *Moby-Dick* look like *Free Willy*. Under the command of Captain George Pollard Jr, the twenty-one crew members set sail on what was supposed to be a two-and-a-half-year trip to fuck up some whales off the west coast of South America. The crew included kids and teenagers, and one boy – the captain's cousin – named Owen Coffin, which is an omen if ever I saw one.[36] If you're putting together a voyage to the most dangerous parts of the seas, hold a few more interviews until you find someone called Ian Floatsquitewell rather than Johnny Corpse, that's my advice. Play it safe.

Within a few days, the trip was going badly. The ship had been hit by bad weather and nearly sank, destroying one of the sails and irreparably damaging two smaller whaleboats. The crew began to think the voyage was cursed, citing recent comet sightings, swarms of locusts and glimpsings of a sea serpent.

The voyage soon picked up though, and the crew began some whale slaughter, before stopping off in the Galápagos to stock up on tortoises to eat, in the strange belief that tortoises could go without food or water for over a year. I'm guessing that a lot of these whalers owned dogs as children that mysteriously got thinner and thinner before 'going to live on a farm'. Loaded full of tortoises that were about to starve to death, the crew of arseholes set sail once more, when disaster struck. In the whaling grounds, thousands of miles off the west coast of South America, a whale rammed into the *Essex* while most of the crew were out whaling on smaller whaling boats. The whale then went on its way, probably quite pleased with itself, having just fucked up the mothership. The ship, meanwhile, began to sink.

The crew salvaged what they could from the ship, including navigation charts, and got back into their tiny whaling vessels. To their west they realised there was a small group of islands about 1,200 miles away, which wasn't great. To their east was South America, which would require them to sail against the winds for 1,000 miles before turning and travelling another 3,000 miles, which was worse. They opted to go for the second plan, on the grounds that the nearer islands *might have cannibals on them*. Which later, had they been in the mood and not been eating their friends, might have elicited an ironic chuckle.

The crew travelled for weeks, eating the rest of their seawater-soaked food and drinking their remaining fresh water before moving on to, well, let's say human-filtered water. They hit upon a small island, where they nommed on pretty much all of the food supplies within a week. Three of the crew members opted to remain on the island and take their chances, while the seventeen others set sail once more.

This time they started dying of thirst and hunger. The first two to die were given a burial at sea, but the third was kept on board one of the boats, where the body lay like an elephant in the room, by which I mean it was technically edible. After a brief chat about whether everyone was up for a bit of cannibalism – the sort of situation where nobody wants to be the first to say 'yes' – the crew agreed to start eating the body. Four days later, their regular food supplies ran out. Now I don't want to get judgy, but why were they dining on human flesh before they'd run out of tins of beans and sticky toffee pudding? I don't know why, but if someone was forced to eat my corpse I feel like it would be disrespectful to then move on to a tiramisu. I realise the situation was unusual, but in lieu of a decent send-off I'd at least take not being a starter.

The new system of eating anybody who died worked just fine for a while, until they found themselves in a situation where everybody was hungry but nobody was quite dead enough to be food. In February, well over a month after their ship was destroyed, they agreed to draw lots to decide who should be eaten next. The captain's nephew, little Johnny Coffin, of course drew the black spot, and was killed by his friend, who drew the second black spot. This would make things somewhat awkward were the captain to survive and have to explain to his sister what had happened. When she asked, 'Where is he?', I suspect not even saying 'Oh, he's around' and patting his tummy would lighten the mood.

Eventually a ship came across the boats, where they found the remaining eight men lying exhausted with bleached human bones scattered around them like discarded pizza boxes after a bender. The crew had chomped their way through seven of their mates, surviving thereafter by gnawing on the bones. But at least they'd managed to avoid Cannibal Island (which turned out not to have any cannibals on it at all), as that could have been a fucking disaster.

THERE'S ONLY SO LONG YOU CAN GO WITHOUT TAKING A POO

Serena Williams pushed herself so hard she's won an astonishing twenty-three Grand Slam singles titles. Usain Bolt tested the limits of the human body, proving that it was possible to run 100m in just 9.58 seconds. Lamar Chambers went forty-seven days without taking a poo.

On 17 January 2018, London-born Lamar was pulled over following a brief car chase. When police approached the 24-year-old's car he was allegedly seen eating something, which officers thought were drugs and he claimed was just some delicious chicken. To be fair, if you've just been in a car chase you can probably do with a mouthful or two of comfort food.

He was placed in a cell with a 'modified toilet', which is to say you poo into the bowl and have no option to flush. Now most of you might think 'game over' at this point, and confess – 'Yes, OK, I did eat a little bit of cocaine.' Not Lamar. There were two things he refused to do, and they were quit and shit. With the dedication and determination of Rocky running up the stairs in *Rocky*, Chambers decided to hold it in. Cue a montage of him sitting in a cell to 'Eye of the Tiger', but instead of punching some meat he's trying not to strain.

Lamar held it in for fifteen days before the police started tweeting about his bowel movements, drawing huge attention from the press and adding pressure to an already quite pressured situation. The absolute hero was still eating and drinking at this time, packing it all down, and probably asking the guard to google 'If you don't poo for ages do you poo out your mouth?'

Time went on, and the police became concerned about his wellbeing. They were convinced he had swallowed drugs – the cessation of defecation for several weeks is unusual, even if you have a phobia of shitting chicken. But they didn't want him to die, which, shockingly, is a possibility. Just as it's possible to shit yourself to death, you can not shit yourself to death.

One man in Australia in 2018, for instance, lost all feeling in his legs and nearly died, courtesy of a gigantic poo that had been building up inside him over the course of several weeks. He finally sought hospital treatment when his legs were cold to the touch and he could no longer move them. His faeces had become so impacted and backed up it had distended his large intestine and put pressure on his right iliac artery. It was this pressure that caused the pain in his leg, as well as the paralysis. They had to perform surgery to remove the poo, but it was still thirteen days before he could walk again.

He was actually lucky. In 2015 a teenage girl with a phobia of toilets died after holding in a bowel movement for eight weeks.[37] The build-up led to her chest cavity becoming compressed and eventually she died of a heart attack.

The record for not doing a number two in police custody was thirty-three days before Lamar went in. He managed to hold it in, risking his own life and toilet when he got home, for a whopping month and a half. The police dropped charges due to 'insufficient evidence',[38] forced to concede that they couldn't prove beyond reasonable doubt that he hadn't just been holding it in as part of, say, a science experiment to see if it would make its way out of his mouth.

What reward did our hero get, the man who pushed his body to the absolute limit and whose persistence finally made me feel like a patriot? After being released and taken to the hospital and treated for his impacted faeces, he was immediately rearrested on suspicion of being involved in the supply of a Class A drug. He had held in a gigantic shit for longer than any other human on record for no benefit whatsoever.

HUMAN DECANTING

Now I don't want to come across as an old fuddy-duddy, but as a general rule I firmly believe it's best to treat your penis as a one-way system. Things come out, and only very rarely and on precise instruction of a doctor should things go back up. None of this hanging out in rivers where worms swim up there, or just plain getting bored when left too long in a room with a pen. Play it safe. If in doubt, things only come out. But it seems I am completely alone in my 'don't put stuff up there' campaign, while you all go around ramming things in there like you're refilling a Pez. In a practice I learned about from a friend and I'm going to repeat to you as some sort of therapy for me, people are reportedly acting as 'human decanters' at those 'sex orgies' they have these days.

How does this work? Well, one person gets a bottle of wine, itself already a perfectly acceptable way of storing wine, and a catheter. They take the catheter and ram it up inside the penis all the way into the bladder, in order to drain it. Now the bladder's empty, it's time to get the Merlot. Through highly complex methods I won't go into in case you perverts give it a try (imagine squeezing a Capri-Sun into a vole and you're basically there, to be fair), you get the wine from where it was, up the penis and into the new home: your bladder. Gone are the notes of oak and rose, to be replaced with notes of ammonia and asparagus.

Now I know what you're thinking: at this stage of proceedings you are merely a human bottle. Well, you absolute pedant, this is only temporary because as a human decanter it is your job to go and urinate into the glasses of the guests for their consumption. While a novelty I'm sure, I can pretty much guarantee that what you've gone and done is turn a fine chardonnay into a chardonnay-piss spritzer.

Anyway, to really ram home (like a catheter going into a penis) why you shouldn't do this – other than that modern wine doesn't need decanting anyway and maybe just have a coke – there's evidence of the damage it can do to your body. See, I didn't want this one to be true either. I'm someone who is basically desperate to learn something horrible so that I can write about it, but even I have my limits. And apparently that limit is people at parties using other people as bottles. But after the most careful google of my life, it turns out there's at least one medical report of a man who ended up with injuries resulting from the practice. A man in his twenties was admitted to ICU with a kidney infection and septic shock, where he had to patiently explain to someone who'd put in years of hard work to become a doctor that he was paid to be a human wine bottle, which is probably more humiliating than pissing wine.[39]

00 KITTY

The problem with spying is that it doesn't take long for the other side to figure out how they're being spied on, necessitating both sides to think up increasingly unhinged ways to spy on each other. In one particularly gruesome example of this, in the 1960s the CIA decided to shove some recording equipment in a cat.

It's testament to the CIA's 'no idea is a bad idea' work culture that somebody felt comfortable enough to say – like Q pitching gadgets to Bond – 'Let's crack open a cat's skull and ram a microphone up there, try and train it to spy on the commies,' and nobody called HR with 'concerns about Alan'. In fact, it sparked a five-year research project, as a result of which they implanted a microphone in the cat's ear canal and a radio transmitter in its skull or tail, depending on whose testimony from the project you listen to. The plan was to train a *cat* to get close enough to targets to listen in on their conversations.

After half a decade of research on how to turn a cat into a spy, they came across an obvious problem: the cat wouldn't listen to a single fucking instruction it had been issued. At no point during their research, apparently, did anyone stop and think, 'Ah now, hang on a second. Maybe we could concentrate on mastering simple instructions like "eat this cat food brand you actively enjoyed yesterday" before we move on to "spy on Soviet Russia".'

'They found he would walk off the job when he got hungry,' ex-CIA officer Victor Marchetti said.[40] They ended up finding a way of dealing with the cat's hunger through operating on it (which I'm imagining meant the cat equivalent of a gastric band), rather than doing something radical like feeding it food.

Finally, miked up, 'trained' and ready for its first mission, the cat was sent to listen in to a conversation between two men in a park near the Soviet compound in Washington, DC. It was released nearby and, according to Marchetti, was promptly hit by a taxi and killed. The mission was a complete flop, unless they could think up a way to get Soviets to hold all their top-secret meetings near roadkill. Though conflicting reports from Robert Wallace, former Director of the CIA's Office of Technical Service, say that the cat wasn't killed by a taxi but that they gave up when they realised that it's near impossible to get a cat to do anything you want it to do, let alone run around the city like James Bond.

THE TAILOR WHO THREW HIMSELF OFF THE EIFFEL TOWER

You probably won't be surprised to learn that the history of how we went from not having parachutes to having parachutes wasn't exactly blood free. There isn't a huge overlap between people who think 'Reckon I'll strap some cloth to my back and jump off a building' and grounded people who know what the fuck they are doing and want to remain alive.

The parachute had been designed in theory by people throughout history. In eleventh-century England, Eilmer of Malmesbury supposedly attempted flight using wings of his own design, and jumped from the top of Malmesbury Abbey.[41] He claimed as an old man that he had flown for several hundred metres, but he actually ended up falling to the ground and snapping both his legs, permanently putting them out of use, so ultimately that's not a great brag. He attributed his failure to 'forgetting to provide himself a tail' rather than not having a clue what he was doing, and honestly I kind of respect him more for not learning a thing as his bones cracked from jumping off a church.

It would take until 26 December 1783 for someone to successfully land using a parachute. Louis-Sébastien Lenormand jumped from the tower of the Montpellier observatory on Boxing Day, using a 14ft parachute with a rigid wooden frame to slow his fall, probably prompting a relative to ask, 'Are you sure you liked that Christmas sweater I bought you? It's just that I got you it and then the very next day you jumped off a fucking building.'

Soon after that, in 1785, Jean-Pierre Blanchard proved that the parachute could be used from greater heights, by throwing his dog out of a hot air balloon attached to a parachute. Being a science man, or maybe just some sort of dog-hating arsehole, he continued to throw his dog out of a hot air balloon to check the safety of the 'chute. In 1793, however, he claimed his hot air balloon blew a puncture and he was forced to jump out of it himself using the parachute, though there were zero witnesses to this and it's hard not to think he pretended he'd done it after people gave him shit for being a lot wussier than his dog.

Fast forward to Franz Reichelt, my favourite of all the people strapping cloth to themselves and then jumping off a thing. Franz was a tailor who was clearly bored by making regular dresses and decided to create one that could fly. In 1910 he designed something that looked not unlike a modern-day wingsuit, though a lot baggier and less likely to actually slow a deadly descent. The best way I can describe it is if, instead of picturing a flying squirrel, you picture a regular squirrel that has piled on the pounds and then lost it all after conquering his addiction to acorns, leaving *some* skin flaps, sure, but not nearly enough to achieve flight. Reichelt began testing his suits using mannequins, but try as he might they kept smashing against the floor in a way which would clearly be fatal to humans. He decided that the problem was that the drop was too short and he'd need to go much higher for his suit to suddenly start defying the laws of physics.

On Sunday, 4 February 1912, he booked a slot at the Eiffel Tower to test his suit.[42] Turns out back then you could book a trip up it for any old shit like this. 'Can you book me in for a 9 a.m. jumping?' 'Sorry sir, all booked up. Can I tempt you with a 10 a.m. standing too close to the edge and feeling a bit woozy?' His friends tried to convince him to throw a mannequin instead, not even considering the possibility of lobbing some dogs off there, but Franz couldn't be convinced. They then started telling him about the wind speed in an attempt to get him to cancel, before mentioning his many, many failures to get it to work with a mannequin. He told his friends, 'You are going to see how my

74

seventy-two kilos and my parachute will give your arguments the most decisive of denials.'

At 8.22 a.m., watched by a crowd of journalists and the public, as well as several cinematographers he had hired, he stood on a stool placed upon a table, hesitated for around forty seconds, and jumped. He plummeted to the ground in far fewer seconds, crushing his right arm and leg, suffering numerous scrapes and bruises to his torso and several cracked ribs, and breaking his skull and spine. Plus he obviously died. During the time that he must have pictured everybody congratulating him on his baller move, members of the public were measuring the depth of the cartoonish hole he'd left in the ground on impact. Which was 15cm, for anybody who's interested.

THERE WAS A CRAZE OF PEOPLE DIPPING THEIR BALLS IN SOY SAUCE

In early 2020, just before everyone learned of 'The Disease', the biggest worry on anyone's mind was the youths attempting to taste soy sauce with their testicles. OK, also the rise of fascism, and poverty, etc., but I really do feel like you're splitting soy sauce-soaked pubic hairs here. In January, one person tweeted 'BALLS HAVE TASTEBUDS, BALLS HAVE TASTEBUDS' over an image of a study that claimed testicles are equipped with taste receptors.

In fact, this bit is true. Taste receptors have been found elsewhere in the body too, including your stomach, lungs, brain and – oh sweet merciful Christ – your anus. '[The] function of taste receptors and signaling proteins outside of [the] taste system is still unclear ... [in some areas] they seem to be part of the chemical sensing of sugars or amino acids,' Bedrich Mosinger, a researcher involved in the study, told *Business Insider* at the time. 'For the most part, though, full function of these extra-orally located taste receptors is unknown.'

The study found that taste receptors, including taste proteins for sweet and umami flavours, are present in the testicles of mice and have a role in their fertility. Without these receptors – when they were taken out of the mice – the rodents became infertile. Their sperm struggled to swim and their testicles became malformed. The internet sort of glossed over this bit and jumped straight to 'Ah yes, I see, I can taste meatballs with my balls'. Before you could say 'At least use cutlery,' people who get their science from a Twitter account yelling 'YOUR BALLS CAN TASTE' began dipping their balls into different foods and drinks to see if they were yummy.

'I can totally taste this, this is so weird,' YouTuber GayGod told his followers after plopping them into a cup of soy. 'I can taste like I had soy sauce, like when you burp up soy sauce. It does kind of sting afterwards, I'm not going to lie.'

'Hold on now, oh my god I can taste the salt,' said one Tik-Tok user whose cojones were covered in soy sauce at the time. 'That's ridiculous.' Others agreed, and before you knew it, there were videos all over the internet of people all claiming that this was a real thing.

So, were they actually tasting the soy sauce and other food-stuffs they were so delicately teabagging for videos? No. They'd been squatting over/slathering themselves with perfectly good soy sauce as if they were a piece of salmon sashimi for no real reason whatsoever. 'The study (or any that have followed) hasn't shown that any animal can actually "taste" via these receptors like we'd taste something from the mouth. There is no scientific or medical evidence to back up claims that men (of any species) can actually taste things through their junk,' Dr Kieran Kennedy told *Men's Health Australia*.[43] 'So while the fact that there might be taste receptors in the testicles is pretty damn interesting, it unfortu-nately doesn't mean (at least unfortunately for TikTok soy sauce users) there's any evidence they can actually taste things.' It's why you never see the judges plonk their testicles in the pudding on *Masterchef.* Even Gregg.

The taste receptors studied in the research, I should add, were found in the testicles and not the scrotum. So what these dippers were doing would be like trying to taste soy sauce the regular way by applying it to the outside of your cheek. And while we're here, I'd like to add that nobody seemed to notice that the study also mentioned that receptors can be found in the anus. As a result, none of them paused to think, 'Ah, now hang on, I don't walk around tasting shit in my mouth the whole time.'

78

THINGS THAT LIVE INSIDE OTHER THINGS

Question: Do you think nature is beautiful? Oh you do, do you? Well congratulations, you just described thirty-two-foot tapeworms that feast off their host before making their way out of said host's anus as beautiful. Feel proud of yourself?

For every cute animal, there are a whole host of parasites (pun accidental but approved in retrospect) that are unimaginably awful. Here's a rundown of some of those horror shows that you, in your stupidity, thought were pretty.

Horsehair worms

Horsehair worms are named for their resemblance to horsehair. If they were named for what they do, they'd have to be named something like 'suicide worms' or 'those cricket-killing cunts', which is probably why they went for 'horsehair worms'.

These parasites begin life as 0.01-inch larvae, emerging from eggs wrapped around water plants. The larvae make their way to the edge of the water, where they attach themselves to grass or other vegetation, at which point they're immediately eaten by crickets. Don't feel bad for them just because they're newborn babies. This is all part of their plan.

Now inside the crickets, the worms begin to bore their way through the wall of their host's gut and into its body cavity, where they can grow up to 2 metres in length, contorting and writhing and digesting their host from the inside.

We're still not at the worst part. In order to be able to breed and continue their horrifying legacy, they need to get back to water. Usually crickets stay away from water, due to not wanting to drown to death. Fair play to them, I may not agree with most of what they cheep but they have some excellent opinions on whether or not drowning is a laugh. When they have these parasites, however, their fear of death seems to disappear, replaced with an irresistible urge to seek out water and leap into it, drowning themselves as soon as is feasible. The worms, which you called beautiful not one page ago, then emerge from their host in order to get busy with other disgusting monsters. It's the CIIIIIIIIIIIRCLE OF LIIIIIIIIIIIFE.

So far, the precise mechanism by which the parasite turns its host into a water-seeking zombie is unknown, but we do know they appear to be producing large amounts of neurotransmitters while they are inside the crickets, which are likely involved in the altered behaviour.[44] In other words they've developed mind-controlling drugs and we don't have a fucking clue how they work, which I find very comforting.

Cymothoa exigua

These bastards are truly bizarre and honestly need to be dealt with before we even think about moving on to cancer. *Cymothoa exigua*, aka the tongue-eating louse, first enter fish through the gills. I'm not sure what it's like to have gills, no matter what the rumours suggest, but I'd imagine it's pretty uncomfortable to have something wriggle into your body through your breathing flaps.

Now inside the fish, they settle down and attach themselves to the gill arches. At some point the male parasites – they all start out as men – can either become female or remain male. If they become female, they will make their way into the mouth of the fish to live the life of a tongue. Once they're in the mouth, they cut off the fish's real tongue using their front claws, and feast on the blood. Using all the tongue blood, they grow larger – to about the size of a fish's tongue. They attach themselves to the stub with their rear hook-like pereopods (let's call them legs to annoy the shit out of biologists) and become a 'pseudo tongue' for the rest of their days, acting as the fish's tongue.[45] Like somebody who murders your accountant but then shows up every year to do your tax returns. In return for performing tongue duties, the louse helps itself to food that the fish eats, causing the fish to lose a bit of weight in the process.

'Oh,' I can hear you say, like the fish-sex crazed person you are, 'but they haven't bred yet, how do they breed?' Calm down, Troy McClure, I'm getting to that part. It's not known for certain where the breeding takes place, but it's definitely within the fish. Either it happens back in the gills, or more likely the male parasites crawl up into the fish's mouth and start banging the tongue.

If you imagine this from the fish's perspective, it truly is horrifying. First, your tongue is gone and that's weird. Then it's back and that's even weirder. But you can't feel it and it's significantly more mobile than you remember. Then suddenly, while you're pondering that, something starts having sex with it.

Fly destroyer
Entomophthora muscae, which somewhat satisfyingly translates as 'fly destroyer',[46] is a fungus which infects a whole bunch of flies.

After a fly has picked up the fungus' spores, it behaves as it normally would for a few days, though those days are now numbered. The fungus is growing inside it, feeding on its innards and taking over its nervous system. On about day four or five, the fly begins to behave oddly. It ceases to fly – at this point it should really hand back its name – before climbing to the top of a nearby object. Once there, it begins shaking violently and spews out some kind of goo – which might be partly fungus and part fly spit – gluing itself in place to the top of the object, essentially making its own gibbet.

Then, at dusk (it's always at dusk), the fly extends its wings upwards painstakingly for over ten minutes, before dying. Now the fungus begins to explode out of the fly's abdomen. High up, the spores can spread, hopefully landing on other flies. But, if that isn't the case, they have a backup. With the dead fly's wings in an upright position and looking much larger than before (which if you were a fly would make you quite randy), male flies have been known to try to have sex with the carcass, getting themselves infected in the process. But at least they won't have to spend many days knowing that they've accidentally done a necrophilia.

IF YOU COVER YOUR NOSE AND MOUTH YOU CAN SNEEZE YOURSELF INTO THE ICU

There are two urban legends that probably stick in your mind about sneezing.

One: If you open your eyes when you sneeze, your eyeballs will pop out like champagne corks. Two: if you sneeze seven times in a row you will do a cum.

Well, you'll be pleased to know that eyes and noses do not work that way. The air spaces in the nose aren't connected to the eye like some sort of meaty spud gun, so there's no way a sneeze or puffing up your cheeks and then smacking them can create the pressure needed to force your eyes out of their sockets and make them dangle around like the ball in a game of swingball. In fact, your eyes closing is a reflex that some people can overcome, and all have gone on to live full eyeball-in-head lives. You *can* vomit so hard that your eye lenses come out, but we'll leave that for another book.[47]

In the same way, the nose is not connected to your genitals, so put down the pepper pot, you aren't going to sneeze yourself to completion. If you sneeze seven times, all it means is you've probably got flu.

The bad news is there are other ways you can severely injure yourself by just having a bit of a sneeze. I sincerely wish I didn't know about it, but I'm now going to tell you here because – fuck you, I guess. I don't see why I should be the only one who's scarred for life.

One 34-year-old man decided to try and stifle a sneeze by holding his nose and covering his mouth at the same time. Why he did this we'll never know. Maybe he was in a situation that needed complete silence and he's a hero of sorts. Maybe his wi-fi went down one day and in the boredom he merely thought, 'Fuck it, I'm going to sneeze internally.'

Upon the attempt, he felt a 'popping sensation' in his neck, which is rarely a sign that things have gone to plan.[48] You never hear top athletes say, 'Yeah, it was a tough race but when I heard that cracking sound in my spine, that's when it all started to come together.' Soon the popping sensation was the least of his problems, because he started feeling a tremendous pain in the throat that prevented him from swallowing. Worse, the sneeze caused a 'change of voice', meaning he had to ask for help in a voice that wasn't his own. Imagine sneezing, you feel a pain and ask for help, and your colleague asks, 'Why the fuck are you talking like Joe Pasquale?'

Doctors soon found that his neck and all the way down to his ribs gave off popping sounds when prodded, a worrying sign that he either had air bubbles inside his deep tissue and muscles or was secretly harbouring two-thirds of the Kellogg's Rice Krispies trio inside his chest cavity – both of which possibilities distress me more than I can explain. A scan showed that he had ruptured the back of his neck – something that is more likely to occur during blunt force trauma than a sneeze – which had caused the air pockets that led to the distressing popping sounds.

The team who treated him noted that halting a sneeze by blocking the nostrils should be avoided, and can lead to everything from a ruptured throat to a cerebral aneurysm. This man thankfully recovered in hospital after being intubated. He was later sent home, but not before his doctors took him aside and advised him to avoid blocking both nose holes and mouth while sneezing, probably while muttering 'You complete fucking nostril' under their breath.

THE WOMAN WHO GAVE BIRTH TO RABBITS

In August 1726, Mary Toft – a 25-year-old woman who worked as a servant in Guildford, Surrey – had a miscarriage. Somewhat unusually, she still looked pregnant a month later. A lot more unusually, she began firing out parts of animals like some sort of meat cannon.[49]

The first thing she gave birth to was a liverless cat, which is remarkable for at least two reasons. One: What was she – not a cat – doing giving birth to a cat? Two: Who the hell witnesses the birth of a cat to a human woman and goes 'FUCK ME, THIS CAT APPEARS TO BE LIVERLESS. ASTONISHING!' as though that was the shocking part.

The family decided to ask for the help of a local physician, which sounds obvious, but part of me wonders if I'd be confused about protocol and think about calling the vet. Guildford obstetrician John Howard visited Mary, and was given the cat that had come from her fanny (something that you'd have to be the most ardent of cat lovers to be pleased about) as well as an assortment of other animal parts. During October, he noted down the various bits of meat that made their way out of her vagina, including the legs of a cat, a rabbit's head and nine dead baby rabbits over the course of just one day.

Not being the most sceptical of doctors, John began writing letters to medics and scientists all over England, telling them about the woman who appeared to be plopping out dead rabbits at a rate at which actual rabbits would be chuffed. He even wrote a letter to the King. And why not. Had I witnessed a pair of cat's legs emerging claw last out of a vagina, I'm sure my first thought would be 'King George I is going to *looooove* this.' Turns out he was right, and King George sent Nathaniel St André, surgeon-anatomist to the King, and Samuel Molyneux, secretary to the Prince of Wales, to investigate. Toft was now a local celebrity, though I'm not sure whether they had enough celebs to have A-listers back in the 1700s, and even less certain where on the scale from Tom Cruise to Cheggers it would make you if your main talent was shooting out Bugs Bunny.

Mary forced out a few more Flopsies in front of her new audience, who then inspected the bodies for clues. The secretary concluded from the organs, rather than the fact that a fucking rabbit had fallen out of her vagina, that they were not created in her womb. The surgeon, meanwhile, was convinced this was the real deal. More doctors got on the case, and came to see her giving birth to more rabbits. The locals were invested in dead rabbits with a zeal that would go unequalled until the creation of Elmer fucking Fudd.

One doctor, Cyriacus Ahlers from Germany, was particularly unconvinced, and demanded to inspect one of the rabbit's anuses. That's one rabbit with one anus, not one rabbit with multiple anuses – that would be plain weird. Up in there, after a bit of rummaging, he found that the rabbit's poo contained corn, which isn't exactly in plentiful supply inside the vag. He had confirmation that something was amiss. He told the King – who I really feel should have had better things to be getting on with than keeping track of Mrs Rabbit Vag – that he believed it to be a hoax. The other doctors were suspicious too, but having spent quite a long time being incredibly on board with the idea, they wanted to keep it a bit quiet that this was anything other than a miracle. André even printed a book about the woman, and the public believed Mary's explanation that her dreams about rabbits and her desire for rabbit meat during pregnancy had turned her into a nerf gun for bunnies.

88

Things got even more out of hand when the national press picked up the story, and people began flocking to see the woman give birth to chunks of meat. André took a gamble on her condition being real, and invited other doctors who were sceptical to come watch her in the act. She was shut away in a bath house in London, far away from any supply of meat. Bizarrely, she still gave birth to rabbits over the course of the next few months, to the surprise of everyone involved. I am, of course, fucking with you. Over the next week, she faded in and out of consciousness due to the various infections that you'd expect to get from acting like a human version of the packaging around a stick of salami.

She was finally busted when it emerged that her husband had been buying a suspicious amount of baby rabbits, some of which her sister had attempted to smuggle to her in the bath house. As you probably guessed from the first sentence, she had been shoving rabbits up there as a prank. Really committing to the bit, she had forced the cat's claws and so many rabbits past her cervix and into her womb.

Toft was quickly forgiven for the hoax, or at least largely forgotten. Giving birth to animals was surprisingly lucrative back then and you can see why they'd do it. For the poor it was probably one of the easiest ways to make money, miles better than becoming a mortgage advisor.

Meanwhile, the medical profession became something of a joke. André in particular was a laughing stock and found himself unable to retain any of his patients. As it turns out, if your surgeon drops into conversation, however casually, that women can give birth to rabbits, even in the 1700s you ask if there's anyone else available to do your colonoscopy.

THE WORST WAY TO DIE

In the twelfth century, an incident known as the Erfurt Latrine Disaster took place, in which between sixty and a hundred nobles died by drowning inside a toilet surrounded by their enemies.[50] (By enemies I mean the other nobles – nobody, to my knowledge, saw faecal matter as their nemesis.)

In July 1184, a dispute grew up between Conrad of Wittelsbach, who was Archbishop of Mainz in what is now Germany, and Ludwig III, who I'd explain a bit more about but you wouldn't get it without seeing Ludwig I and II.

King Heinrich VI decided that he wanted the matter resolved and ordered the parties to come together and sort it out, like your mum sitting you down with your brother only there's a good chance she'd have you executed if you didn't comply. In order to make the meeting successful, he invited a whole buttload of nobles and officials to smooth things over. At no point during any of these invites did the guy even consider the toilet situation, which goes to show you how out of touch kings are. I bet Mario (king of the plumbers) would have stopped briefly to go 'Fifty, fifty-one, fifty-two, fif— ah now, hang on, where's everyone going to poo?' And that thought could have spared dozens of people from a fate worse than death, shortly followed by death.

The room the nobles all crammed into had a weak floor, as they were soon to discover. Falling through a floor would be bad enough at the best of times, but in this case the floor was the only thing separating them and the cesspool below. When this gave way, they plunged into the liquidy shit beneath them, like a hardcore version of *Get Your Own Back* where the gunge is suspiciously brown. Between sixty and eighty people died that day, either in the crush or the excrement. The king and the archbishop survived the meeting as they had gone to discuss matters in an alcove, and

91

were able to hold onto some railings for dear life until rescuers arrived, watching their friends drown in poo-poo to pass the time.

The meeting's location is unclear. Many think it was St Peter's Church. I hope it was of some comfort to the people who died that day that they weren't breathing in any old diarrhoea, but the liquid waste made when holy men ate Holy Communion and subsequently shat out Jesus.

THE MAN WHO WOULDN'T DIE, AND THE PEOPLE WHO WOULDN'T ACCEPT IT

Have you ever heard that riddle that asks 'What happens when an unstoppable force meets an immovable object?' Well, that sort of played out once, but with a guy who wouldn't die and a group of people who really, really just loved trying to murder him.

In 1932, a group of assholes sat down in a New York bar and decided to kill one of the locals. Michael Malloy was a regular drinker at Marino's bar in the Bronx and was always out to get hammered, often passing out on the floor. Nobody really knew anything about him, including himself. He didn't know any of his family, had few friends, and wasn't even sure how old he was, though people guessed he was about sixty. They also knew he was originally from Ireland, though this was likely only due to his accent rather than him actually remembering anything of his life.

Tony Marino, the owner of Marino's, had an axe to grind with Malloy because the guy had several unpaid bar tabs. Unsurprising really: Malloy, a guy who didn't know his own age, doesn't strike me as one who could handle himself in a job interview, let alone hold down a job. What little money he did have came through odd jobs, for which he was often happy to be paid in alcohol (something else that should surely send up a few red flags to HR). If you're thinking that it doesn't follow that Marino would want to murder Malloy because that's sure as hell not going to pay the bar tabs – just hold your horses. Marino and his friends Francis Pasqua and Daniel Kriesberg had a plan.

Marino had experience in the murder-for-insurance-money field, having convinced a homeless woman named Mabelle Carson to take out a policy naming him as a beneficiary (suspicious) and then forcing her to drink alcohol before stripping off her clothes, pouring iced water on her mattress and leaving her next to an open window in the winter, killing her through bronchial pneumonia. He and the others needed something different this time so the cops wouldn't cotton on. Eventually the brains trust came up with a plan: they would simply take out life insurance on Malloy by making him sign the agreement while drunk, the listed beneficiary being 'Nicholas Malloy', then collect it by pretending to be said 'Nicholas Malloy' and kill Michael shortly afterwards.

What? Not all murders can have plotlines from fucking *Poirot*.

Their brilliant plan to make it look like natural causes was to simply give Malloy credit at the bar and let him drink himself to death. The only problem was Malloy wasn't the kind of guy to go down easy. You don't spend years and years being paid in Bacardi Breezers to suddenly die during happy hour.

Malloy pounded drink after free drink, from morning to night, finally crashing in the accommodation his would-be murderers had provided for him out back. Eventually the plotters grew impatient and started plying him with antifreeze instead of booze. Either because he was too hardened by drink by this point or too polite to make a fuss about a free drink, he didn't notice. Or die.

The murder squad grew desperate: they were forking out a hefty sum in insurance payments and free booze, and that's before you factored in the prohibitive cost of antifreeze. They soon moved on to turpentine, then horse liniment, and then just started mixing in rat poison. The man simply would not die.

They eventually tried feeding him wood alcohol, a volatile, colourless, flammable liquid that smells like alcohol but if you drink even 10ml of it you can go permanently blind. They soaked some oysters in the stuff, which even though they were murdering the fuck out of the guy you have to admit was a classy touch, before letting him eat them. Nada. Losing all subtlety, they fed him old sardines in a sandwich filled with poison, carpet tacks and other shrapnel. He asked for a second sandwich.

Sensing the pattern that this guy could eat absolutely anything and get up the next day (like the Terminator, but with food), the gang decided they would freeze him to death. When he passed out one night, they dragged him into the snow and poured five gallons of water onto his chest and face, while he slept there peacefully.[51] When Marino arrived at his bar the next day, Malloy was unconscious in the basement, before waking up and complaining of a mild chill.

Now, with more insurance payments due, they decided to stop beating about the bush and just run him over with a car. They took him outside (while he was passed out again) and had some other arsehole run his car over him. Of course, the first few times Malloy found some unexpected athleticism and leaped out of the way, before finally being struck down. Just to be sure, the car backed over him – lest he get up again and make a pun like 'I'm feeling a bit ... run down' before going on to live into his nineties.

The gang were interrupted and had to leg it before they could check he was dead. For the next few weeks, they had Joseph Murphy, who they'd asked to play Malloy's brother in the event of an insurance payout, ring around the hospitals and morgues asking after him. He was on strict instructions not to shout 'Kerching!' if he found out Malloy was dead.

None of these places had any information on Malloy. Which is bad if your whole plan rests on somebody confirming he's dead for the insurance money. The gang were so desperate, they were talking about complicating matters by killing somebody else to pass them off as Malloy, when Malloy walked into the bar and said 'I sure am dying for a drink.'[52] He remembered nothing of the murder attempt, but had woken up in hospital, where he had been treated for broken bones.

The murder club snapped at this point. On 22 February 1933, they stuck a hose in his mouth and pumped him full of gas, killing him within an hour – which is a long time to sit there gassing someone, with nothing to break the silence other than occasional screams of 'WHY WON'T YOU DIE, YOU FUCK-ING ROBOT?'

Now he was finally dead, they collected the insurance money, before fighting like idiots over the loot. On top of this, rumours spread around the city of 'Rasputin Mike' who refused to die (until he did), which the police picked up on. They had his body exhumed, and it wasn't long before the gang were picked up, put on trial, and sentenced to death. They were all executed on first try, the absolute fucking wimps.[53]

AUSTRALIA, WHERE EVEN THE ADORABLE ANIMALS ARE DICKHEADS

Sooner or later we're all going to have to confront the fact that Australia is uninhabitable. A country where snakes will occasionally pop out of the toilet, but that's not your priority right now because there's a deadly spider eyeing you up, is not a place where humans are meant to live. But we all know about those beasties, so let's take a look at some of the other absolute shits that make Australia such a godawful place to call home.

Magpies

There's a type of magpie (actually a type of passerine known as the butcherbird, which is so much more fitting) that lunges down during something called 'swooping season' to attack the faces of the people below, which they claim is in order to 'protect their young'. A likely story. They've been known to target their victims' eyes, causing numerous injuries that require surgery every year. They've even attacked several people riding bikes, causing them to fall off and die, the cyclists' last thoughts being that they're on a par in the food chain with a worm. As if that isn't bad enough, the birds can remember up to 100 faces and even pick out individual humans they don't like, choosing to attack them continually over the course of several years. 'Magpies seem to have very good memories and have attacked the same people over subsequent seasons,' according to an article in *Magpie Alert!*,[54] which also warns that 'your route belongs to them now'. It advises: 'If it's attacked you before, probably a good idea to use an alternative route next season.'

So that's it. If targeted by a magpie, Australians just accept it and adjust their lifestyle around the nightmare birds. Sorry I'm late, boss, it's just I can't use the highway any more, the fucking magpies won't let me.

Firestarter birds

As well as birds that want to peck your face off, there are three species of bird (at least) that deliberately burn down forests and spread wildfires.

Fire hawks – whose name should have set off alarm bells when they first introduced themselves – were known to indigenous Australians for thousands of years, but only in 2016 did scientists document the birds' alarming behaviour when they took the unprecedented step of actually listening to the aforementioned Australians. The hawks will take sticks that are on fire (due, say, to a lightning strike, which is common in the Northern Territory) and transport them to other areas of dry grassland to deliberately start a fire. This fresh fire will flush out terrified rodents and insects. Just when the little animals are feeling relief that they haven't been killed by fire, they realise they are now bird food.

These arseholes will do the same thing during wildfires too, which could explain why wildfires suddenly jump roads or other natural breaks.[55] I'm not saying it's always their fault, but I don't think the papers should automatically rule out on occasion running the headline 'Dickhead arsonist birds help fuel devastating forest fires to secure buffet'.

The suicide plant

Australia is so awful that even the plants have evolved to be wankers. Of the many stinging trees of this fine country, the Gympie-Gympie is by far the most toxic.

Amongst the first to come across the tree was North Queensland road surveyor A.C. Macmillan. In 1866 he reported that his packhorse had been stung by the tree – which is pretty toxic all over, but especially on the stems – and had then gone insane, dying within hours. Folklore says that having been stung, horses may throw themselves off cliffs in agony.

People who have been stung by the plant describe it as unbearable. 'I remember it feeling like there were giant hands trying to squash my chest,' Ernie Rider said of his encounter in 1963.[56] 'For two or three days the pain was almost unbearable; I couldn't work or sleep, then it was pretty bad pain for another fortnight or so. The stinging persisted for two years and recurred every time I had a cold shower.'

It's so horrendous in fact, that the British, who inhabit an island where it's just the general population you have to be mindful of, considered weaponising it. It's easy to see why; an ex-serviceman in the Australian army claimed that an officer he knew had mistakenly used a leaf of the tree as toilet paper. Thinking he was going to have the familiar feeling of a nice clean anus, he was instead given the most unbearable anus pain he'd ever encountered, and shot himself rather than bear it any longer. Seems a fairly effective weapon to me.

WE KNOW ABOUT TOOTH CAVITIES THROUGH ONE OF THE MOST GROTESQUE EXPERIMENTS IMAGINABLE

Dentists get a lot of stick for being doctors who realised they were too thick for the whole body when they hadn't even made it lower than the face. Mainly by me. But dentists have to do just as much science as everyone else, if only on a tiny portion of the head. One thing that you probably haven't thought about much, because it's something you've just been told your whole life, is that sugar will rot your teeth. But dentists had to figure it out all by themselves, bless them. How they found out is one of the most horrifying things you'll ever come across, so if you dislike dentists, prepare to have all of your suspicions and biases confirmed.

In 1945, we knew a lot about the world. Smoking causes cancer. What we perceive as the force of gravity arises from the curvature of space and time. Cats are just a shit breed of dog. But we knew fuck all about teeth, probably due to the aforementioned laziness of a profession that loses all interest just below the chin. Humanity *highly suspected* that sugar consumption was linked to cavities and tooth decay, but there was no proof. A team of dentists in Sweden decided to change that, and just to make sure that there were no obvious biases to the study, teamed up with the sugar industry to make it happen.

The problem was, as with pretty much any health problem, you can't just give people endless amounts of harmful things like sugar or cigarettes or gallons of unleaded petrol to see how it plays out. Scientists got around this by using the clever trick of being arseholes. Between 1947 and 1949, having had their study approved by the medical board, they fed absurd amounts of sugar to mental patients to see what would happen.

As well as all the money, the sugar industry provided chocolates, sweets and caramels, like an alternative Willy Wonka who was still up for endangering the lives of people in his care, but without the creepy pervert vibes or singing slaves. For two whole years, the patients – mainly people with learning disabilities, aged between fifteen and seventy – were fed copious amounts of sugar. The patients were not being treated particularly well at the Vipeholm Mental Institution either: there were no activities to keep them occupied, and if they were too 'troublesome', they were bathed in cold water.[57] It's pretty grim to think that the monotony was only broken by the occasional scientist who wanted to ruin your teeth to benefit people who weren't you. Two years in, 50 of the 660 subjects had had their teeth destroyed by the sugar,[58] and also picked up other health problems that occur when you eat flumps instead of rice.

Perhaps unsurprisingly, the study didn't come out until several years afterwards. Essentially, the sugar industry and dentists had destroyed the teeth of mentally ill people in order to find out whether or not sugar destroyed teeth, then decided they were cool with it for years afterwards. One of its authors defended the study, fifty years later, saying, 'One, the end sometimes justifies the means, and two, it is easy to be wise after the event.' Who could have known that feeding people with mental disabilities products you suspect will harm them will actually harm them.

THE DANSE REALLY FUCKING MACABRE

In 1940 in Key West, Florida, a young boy looked through the window of a neighbour's house and saw a man dancing with what looked like a woman in their home. He didn't know it right then, thankfully, but he was witnessing one of the most fucked-up dances of all time, and I say that as somebody who has lived through the godless age of the Macarena.

For years Carl Tanzler had had dreams of an attractive dark-haired woman who would become the love of his life. After leaving his wife in 1926 the German-born radiologist moved to Florida, where he posed as a doctor and finally met the woman he believed to be the one. Unfortunately, being a doctor in a hospital, he met her in his capacity of discovering that she'd soon be dead.

Elena De Hoyos had been diagnosed with tuberculosis, which at the time was highly deadly. Wanting to save the woman of his dreams, Tanzler spared no expense in trying everything he could to save her. You don't have visions of the love of your life only to go 'Fuck it, bag her' the second you find out she's ill. He created home-made tonics and medicines, snuck out X-ray machines to take to her home to help with treatment, and bought her far too many gifts to be appropriate from a doctor. He professed his love to Elena many times over, but found it quite unrequited. Despite all his efforts, on 25 October 1931, she died. At which point Tanzler thought 'Next best thing . . .' and decided to marry her corpse.

Tanzler paid for the funeral on behalf of her family, and for a mausoleum to house the body. A touching gesture only undone by the fact that he secretly had the only key. My advice to anyone out there is that if a generous benefactor donates a place to store a relative's body, do a bit of background research to check whether they wish to retain access to the remains.

For two years, Tanzler would visit Elena's resting place every single night, eventually leading to him being fired from his job. It turns out that, while there's no explicit line in the Hippocratic oath forbidding you from visiting the corpse of a patient you've fallen in love with, it's very much against the spirit of the thing. Unfortunately, being fired created a lot of free time for a man who was quite partial to hanging out with a rotting carcass. (Side note, but who knows how many complete wrong 'uns have been prevented from doing heinous crimes simply because they had a lot on.)

It was around this time that he suddenly stopped visiting the mausoleum every night, which Elena's family took to be suspicious, given his previous devotion. They were right to be, seeing as he had gone down to collect her corpse – like a fucked-up Deliveroo – and transported it back to his 'laboratory', where he set about mummifying her body. Given that the body had been decaying for two years now, this would have been a tough job even for some creep who knew what they were doing, but Tanzler had the advantage of having incredibly low standards for what he was looking for in a dead girlfriend. He stuffed her with plaster of Paris, supported her with wires, added glass eyes, and used mortician's wax to try and mould what used to be her flesh into something resembling a face. He lived with her for several years like this, stuffing her full of more rags as her flesh further degraded, and buying her gifts of perfume, which, given the stench, surely must have been a hint.

All the while, the neighbourhood began to get suspicious. For a man who kept to himself and lived, apparently, alone, Tanzler had been buying an awful lot of female clothing and gifts. Then there was the sighting of him dancing with something inside his house. Something which looked more like a doll than a human.

The family finally figured out what had happened and in

October 1940 went around to confront him. Lord knows why it took them until 1940, though I'd hazard a guess that at least a few months were spent trying to brainstorm how to raise the topic of 'So, uh, have you been sleeping with my dead sister's corpse, or . . .?' When Elena's sister entered his house, Tanzler was more than happy to show her his creation. At this point the body looked like a wax figure which he had dressed up in a wedding dress. Look, I'm not defending the guy, but you don't go to the trouble of exhuming your obsession's corpse *not* to perform a creepy marriage ceremony once you've got her home.

The authorities quickly figured out that the doll was actually a heavily decomposed Elena. Among all the other horrifying details, they discovered he had inserted a paper tube inside her, to serve as a makeshift vagina. Despite asking the judge if he could have the body back, and let's just call it 'the tube', he walked away from the ensuing trial a completely free man. The statute of limitations for his crimes – grave-robbing and abusing a corpse – had expired, and everyone learned a valuable lesson: If you're going to become obsessed with a patient, rob her grave, do taxidermy and pretend marry her corpse and then defile it, sure as hell better do so over the course of seven or eight years so that no court in the land can convict you.

THE DAY SOME LIGHT CLOUDS NEARLY CAUSED A NUCLEAR WAR

For someone too young to be around during the Cold War, it strikes me as terrifying that you were all doing drills in case international relations broke down and a nuclear bomb went off (step 1: Get under a table; step 2: Die under the table). If that was you, then I'm glad you lived to see the day that the exact same fear could be evoked over a Donald Trump tweet.

The threat of full nuclear war thankfully never came to fruition, but there were some extremely close calls. You've probably heard of the Cuban Missile Crisis, when there was a tense stand-off between the US and the Soviet Union over their decision to deploy Soviet missiles to Cuba, but there's another incident you may not have heard of, even though it could have resulted in the destruction of much of the world, leading to a post-apocalyptic Earth where radioactive cockroaches hunted mutant humans for meat.

On 26 September 1983, just after midnight in a secret bunker just south of Moscow, a siren began to wail. Sirens aren't great at the best of times, but when your secret bunker happens to be the Serpukhov-5 nuclear early-warning facility, I'd imagine the first thing to follow on the list of protocols upon hearing it is to shit yourself with gusto. Lt. Colonel Stanislav Petrov heard the siren, and saw the single, needlessly sinister word on the screen across the room from him: LAUNCH.[59] The Soviet Union's Oko launch-detection satellites had detected an incoming intercontinental ballistic missile, launched from the United States. 'An alarm went off,' Petrov told the BBC years later.[60] 'It was piercing, loud enough to raise a dead man from his grave.'

Protocol told him he had to report the missile to his superiors, and they would have swiftly followed this with an order to nuke the crap out of the US in retaliation. It's no exaggeration to say that billions of lives were at stake that day, once you factor in a nuclear winter. Had he lost his cool, or reported exactly what he saw, all those lives would have been lost.

He picked up the phone and informed his superiors that the missile was a false alarm, believing it to be a bug. He figured it wouldn't make sense for the US to only launch one missile rather than overwhelm the Soviet Union with force, making sure they couldn't strike back.

The computer then reported another missile, and another, and another, all headed right at Stanislav and his presumably ruined trousers. Worse, it was estimated that they would arrive within twelve minutes, giving him virtually no time to act and/or mop. The computer reported that the probability of a strike was 100 per cent.

Fortunately for the world, Stanislav was a bit of a Luddite. Not a full 'smash the looms' Luddite, but distrustful of the new computer system, which was telling him he was about to snuff it.[61] He picked up the phone and again told his superiors that it was a false alarm, preventing a retaliatory attack. Even then, he wasn't sure. 'The thought crossed my mind that maybe someone had really launched a strike against us,' he told the BBC. 'That made it even harder to lift the receiver and say it was just a false alarm.'

It's a good job they didn't retaliate, as the satellites were actually picking up sunlight reflected off some high-altitude clouds, and it would have been a bit of a dick move to retaliate with hundreds of nuclear missiles in response to a bit of weather. Boy, would their faces have been red, and then nuked off.

Through keeping a cool head and reasoning that the US was unlikely to launch a pre-emptive nuclear attack at that time, Petrov saved billions of lives at great personal risk. If he'd been wrong (and managed to survive the apocalypse) he would have been executed for his mistake. As it was, there was an inquiry into the incident, after which he was scapegoated. He was moved out of the way of any real duties, and lived out his life in obscurity for decades before the story came out, suffering a nervous breakdown in the interim. All for having the cheek to save mankind from total fucking nuclear annihilation.

FARTING WAS ONCE
A VIABLE CAREER OPTION

Comedy has moved on through the years, from those fabled times when early cave people saw someone else getting fucked up with a big club and giggled because it wasn't them. We've been through the 'jester' phase, the 'women bending over while a swanny whistle sounds' phase, and sadly we're not yet over the 'Mrs Brown's Boys' phase. One man is even said to have died laughing after comparing the prices of stock commodities of 1915 to those of 1920, when he laughed so much he gave himself heart failure.[62] Still, he had a good innings. Thank Christ nobody showed him their tax returns before he'd even turned twenty-three.

And of course we had the farting age, which seems to have endured for centuries. Roland the Farter was given 30 acres of land by King Henry II for performing 'Unum saltum et siffletum et unum bumbulum'[63] (one jump, one whistle and one fart) every Christmas for the family, which may go some way to explain why his son King Richard I was so fucked up. I'm not saying I'm perfect at raising children, but I've read the manuals and on pretty much page 1 it says 'no inviting strange men around to fart right at your kids'.

This musical art form has disappeared at various times

throughout history, despite the obvious advantages of the instrument's portability compared to, say, a cello. It was rediscovered independently – it's not like you can get grade five in expelling flatulence – by a teenager named Joseph Pujol in the late 1800s.

Pujol was in the sea one day, seeing how long he could hold his breath underwater, when he felt an odd sensation in the butthole region as well as his stomach. He clambered back to dry land a bit freaked out, like Spider-Man after being bitten by a radioactive spider, before seeking a quiet spot on the beach. Here he learned the nature of his superpower as he shat out two litres of water onto the sand.[64] He visited the kind of doctor who thought nothing of it and told him not to go in the sea.

Decades of wasted years went by before, upon recounting his anecdote to some friends about that time he sucked up then shat out water, they egged him on to try it again. In front of his chums he tried the feat once more, plunging his anus beneath the water, sucking the water into his anus and shitting it out again, as their astonished faces filled with wonder.

Most people would have left it there, but not Pujol, who decided to turn this ability into a career. He began practising and discovered he could do the same thing with air instead of water by bending himself over and sucking in his diaphragm while holding his breath.[65] Over several years, he perfected his art, until he was able to change pitch and volume and perform impressions of owls, ducks, bees, roosters, toads, a dog that had got its tail stuck in a door, and other people farting. He took his show on the road under the name Le Pétomane, which sounds classy in French but translates as 'the Fartomaniac'. Soon he was auditioning at the Moulin Rouge nightclub in Paris in 1892. Nervously he cleansed his 'instrument' by sucking up water into his butthole the way

Celine Dion would gargle before a performance. The owner was blown away (Oh, you're judging me for making a fart joke in a chapter about farting, are you? Take a long hard look at yourself) and hired him immediately. A guy comes in and starts farting 'La Marseillaise' at you, you don't mess around with playing the negotiations cool. He ended up earning 20,000 francs for some of his shows, where he'd fart at the audience to their delight, before moving on to other aspects of farting, such as blowing out a candle with a fart and inserting a tube into his anus with a lit cigarette on the end before blowing smoke rings. He was much loved and even performed in front of the King of Belgium.

It wasn't to last for ever though. He got into a legal dispute with the owner of the Moulin Rouge after he was found outside farting in front of a cookie stand in an attempt to help a friend sell cookies. Which is a business plan you so rarely see these days, because, frankly, Greggs are cowards. The owner argued that he was only allowed to fart in the club, which was quite a big ask, like if your own employer asked you to only do a poo between the hours of seven and nine in the morning. He was replaced, as if the tale wasn't weird enough, by a female farter who turned out to be cheating by using bellows tucked between her legs.

FINDING ALIEN LIFE COULD MEAN WE'RE DOOMED

Finding aliens would either be amazing or time to evacuate the White House, according to the films. We're either going to have wacky adventures, or be wiped out by gooey psychos unless Will Smith can help it. There are many reasons why we might or might not want to find advanced aliens – what if they wanted to turn our skin into shoes, or didn't think we were cool – but there are also reasons why we might not want to meet even simple life-forms. Even finding them with a rover millions of miles away could signify our doom. It all has to do with the Fermi Paradox and the Great Filter.

The Fermi Paradox

You probably know about the Fermi Paradox, but for those of you who don't, here's a refresher. Given the high probability that alien life exists out there in the universe, why the hell has nobody got in touch? If there are so many others out there, possibly at far more advanced stages of civilisation than we are because of how long the universe has dragged on for (no offence, universe, but get to the point. What was with that several billion years when everything was just soup?), why are they not doing what we're doing, sending out probes willy-nilly and desperately searching for other signs of life?

Think of it like you wake up on an island with no memory. Nature around you is teeming with life. You have no way of knowing whether there's anybody else out there. You suspect there must be – it would be weird if it was only you and Tom Hanks in existence (there's always a Tom Hanks) – so why has nobody swum here? Are they too far away? Did everyone else on the planet die before they could be arsed to build a boat?

The Great Filter

One theory is the Great Filter. The hypothesis goes that before alien civilisations can make it to the point where they are able to leave their solar system and begin colonising their galaxy, something happens to prevent them from doing so, or we'd see evidence for advanced life teeming in our galaxy. Which we don't. Please feel free to insert your own joke here about not finding intelligent life on Earth.

Whether this occurs at the step from multi-cell life to animals that can use tools, or from where we are now to exploring the galaxy, we just don't know. What makes it so interesting (and a little bit terrifying) is we wouldn't know if we are past the Great Filter or whether it's going to happen in our future. Could it be that most alien life-forms don't make it past single-cell life, and we have made it past the filter? Or at some point yet to come are we, like other alien civilisations out there, about to destroy ourselves before we are able to leave Earth, perhaps through war, using up our resources before we can escape, or voluntarily evolving back into fish?

In terms of you on your island, it means you don't know

whether other people are out there and will show up any minute, are still developing the technology to cross oceans having got stuck on the pedalo, or whether they have long since died out, perhaps in some sort of pedalo incident. If you could find out clues, say a blood-soaked pedalo, or even something a little less on the nose, you might be able to figure out your own chances of developing the technology needed to go and explore other islands and continents.

Here's where it gets a bit doomy. Because, if the Great Filter is correct, it means that we can learn things from any life that we *do* find, say on Mars. Oxford University philosophy professor Nick Bostrom says that he hopes the search for extra-terrestrial life turns up nothing. If we found very simple life-forms, Bostrom argued in an article published in the *MIT Technology Review* in 2008, then we could conclude that the filter happens some time *after* that point of life.[66] If we found multicellular life, this would narrow down the likely point at which the Great Filter could take place to after *that* form of life developed. Say you're sat on your island and a rubber ring shows up, without even a dead person inside it manning the thing. This would tell you that life elsewhere has at least developed the technology to have pool parties, but not to cross oceans with their party gear. This, combined with the fact that *nobody* has shown up yet, tells you your idea of building a luxury yacht might be a tad on the unrealistic side, even if Tom Hanks would put down that football you're fairly sure he's been making sex eyes at and fucking concentrate.

Bostrom believes that in order to narrow down where the filter takes place, we should look at life on Earth to see which steps are improbable. 'One criterion is that the transition should have occurred only once,' he wrote. 'Flight, sight, photosynthesis, and limbs have all evolved several times here on Earth, and are thus ruled out.'

He also argued that evolutionary features that took a long time to occur even after prerequisites were met would indicate that this evolutionary step, e.g. the original emergence of life, was improbable. The step from animals to humans took place over a relatively short time period, geologically speaking, which suggests it's a weak candidate for a Great Filter event. Given a lot more time, we might find ourselves chatting away to cats.

If we were to find evidence of vertebrates on Mars (we won't, but still) he believed that it would be terrible news, as it would suggest that the bulk of the Great Filter is still in our future, and we'll have to face the probability that we will go extinct before we are technologically mature enough to travel through the galaxy. 'Such a discovery would be a crushing blow. It would be by far the worst news ever printed on a newspaper cover,' Bostrom wrote. 'This is why I'm hoping that our space probes will discover dead rocks and lifeless sands on Mars, on Jupiter's moon Europa, and everywhere else our astronomers look. It would keep alive the hope for a great future for humanity.'

So, though there are many other possible solutions to the Fermi Paradox that are worth looking at – if you enjoy that sort of thing – if Bostrom is correct it means that finding evidence of advanced civilisations is good news, but finding the wrong stages of life that evolved independently in our own solar system would be the worst possible news we could receive. Leaving you sat all alone on your island, knowing at some point that you and Tom Hanks are going to twat each other to death.

THE WEIRDEST MARATHON IN HISTORY

119

In 1904, the Olympic Games were hosted in St Louis, the first time they were staged in America, and coinciding with the World's Fair taking place in the same city. The Games were completely overshadowed by the fair, in fact, due to it hosting its own sporting events. It's like putting *The X Factor* on at the same time as whatever the hell that other show is that people who watch *The X Factor* prefer.

The World's Fair had a lot of grim features that would age incredibly poorly. The worst bit was the 'human zoo', in which they brought 'savages' from around the world and let them carry out normal day-to-day activities while people gawped at them like they were in a regular actual zoo. As a crossover event with the Olympics, the (non-athlete) participants were recruited for an 'Anthropology Days' event in which they participated in normal events like the long jump and javelin, before being made to climb up greased poles and throw mud at each other. After which the event's organiser concluded that 'the savage has been a very much overrated man from an athletic point of view'.[67]

The main thing the games are remembered for, however, is the marathon – the weirdest one in history.

It took place in the blazing sun on a scorching road. Most of the participants were amateurs, and many of them hadn't even competed in a marathon before that day. For some reason the organisers picked this year to test the effects of dehydration,[68] perhaps thinking it might spice things up a bit if the mounting corpses of dehydrated runners could be used as hurdles. As such, they wouldn't give out any water along the way, except at two stations. This move wiped out more than half the field, who were forced to leave the race because several of them were on the edge of being dead. There were professionals that took part in the race, but most of them didn't fare any better, forced as they were by the organisers into turning the noble sport of Ancient Greece into Wacky Races.

When the marathon kicked off they all ran down the road, which was still functioning *as* a road. They were forced to dodge past carriages and weave through people just out for a ramble, making it less a challenge of endurance and more a challenge of seeing who was impolite enough to tell pedestrians to get the fuck out of their way. The roads were so dusty that American runner William Garcia collapsed requiring surgery, after the coarse dust he'd swallowed ripped open his stomach lining.

The winner of the race (briefly) was an American. He was being given his gold medal when a witness told the officials he had given up less than halfway and been given a lift to the finishing line.

Meanwhile, any athletes that could possibly have been able to win the race without using a car weren't having a great time. One entrant, Len Tau, was chased a mile off course by wild dogs, before finally losing them and correcting course. He came in a respectable ninth. The Cuban entrant, who wore a dress shirt and formal trousers as he'd forgotten his gear, became waylaid when he stopped off to go scrumping. The apple he nicked from beside the road was rotten, and he gave himself food poisoning, after which he made the decision to nap for a while at the roadside. You'd think he'd know what consistency you're supposed to look out for in apples, himself being a fucking melon. The nap slowed the actually quite good runner, but he still managed to scrape his way back to finish fourth. It was basically the parable of the tortoise and the hare, except the hare wasn't too hot on food hygiene and ended up shitting itself into second place.

The ultimate winner, Thomas Hicks, meanwhile, was completely off his tits on rat poison he'd taken as a performance-enhancing drug.[69] Worse, he was feeling rough throughout the whole race and, since he was denied water, his team started feeding him brandy and egg whites mixed with more rat poison (which perked him up no end). By the time he was ready to win the race, he was hallucinating that the finish line was 20 miles away, and he collapsed just before it. He was carried to the ribbon by his trainers, at which point the organisers clearly thought 'You know what? Fuck it, that'll do' and awarded him first place. During his drug-fuelled semi-win, he had lost eight pounds, despite consuming a lot of egg.

A DOCTOR TRIED TO REVIVE GEORGE WASHINGTON LIKE A ZOMBIE BY PUMPING HIM FULL OF LAMB'S BLOOD

These days, having a fear of being buried alive is a bit of a quirk. Very few people (though obviously there are exceptions) actually end up in the ground before they've even bothered to die. But back in George Washington's time, people were very quick to throw you in the dirt before they'd given you the courtesy of a quick 'alright then, hands up anyone who's alive'. It turns out Washington's lifelong fear was misplaced, however. When he said his final words, 'I am just going! Have me decently buried; and do not let my body be put into the vault less than three days after I am dead,'[70] he should have crowbarred in a sentence about not wanting to be pumped full of lamb's blood on a whim.

Washington was suffering from a viral infection of the throat following an ill-advised horse ride on a chilly day. Soon he found he was struggling to breathe, and medical help was sent for. One doctor, who had treated Washington his whole life, arrived along with George Rawlins, an expert in bloodletting – the art of removing someone's blood in a way that at the time they thought was therapeutic, but we now know is more likely to 'make you dead'. Today, this would be like the Prime Minister, laid low with the sniffles, calling for his GP and a guy who's good at twatting people in the testicles with steel toe-capped shoes. Though no doubt enjoyable in terms of the media cycle, it was only ever going to make the situation worse. By nightfall, Rawlins had taken about 40 per cent of his blood. I don't want to get all technical on you, but you need blood to live.

On top of not having blood, he had been brewed a concoction by Colonel Lear, a tonic made from molasses, butter and vinegar, that nearly caused him to choke to death. Maybe this was Washington's bad call for leaving his medicines to a man whose speciality in life, as an army colonel, was making other people dead. He was not in great hands, but fortunately there was another doctor on the way, one who thought (like an absolute maverick for the time) that putting blood *into* the body was actually better for you than granting it its freedom with a big knife. Dr William Thornton was into the idea of transfusions, which until then had endured a chequered history.

You're probably aware that a lot of humans can't transfer blood to humans with a different blood group. Fun fact: a symptom of having been transferred the wrong blood type is 'a feeling of impending doom' which, if left untreated, will actually result in doom.[71] Your body sees the blood as a foreign invader and, like the Home Office flooring it to Dover whenever they hear about a group of vulnerable asylum seekers, will begin to attack its foe.

This adverse reaction, which can often lead to death, is made worse if, say, you got the blood of a horse and injected it into some dude. Early experiments did just this. The first ever attempt, in 1667, involved a French physician giving a boy a transfusion of sheep's blood.[72] He didn't give him much, and the kid miraculously survived, for reasons entirely unrelated to injecting him with stuff that should be inside a sheep. Having one not-dead kid, he chalked it up as a massive win, and decided to replace the entire blood of a mentally unwell man, in the belief that having 'good' blood instead of 'bad' blood might cure him. For some reason, they believed that the good blood should be cow's blood, and set about firing the moo into the likely unwilling patient, who died on the third try.

A century later, the tech and reasoning hadn't moved on much. Blood transfusions had been banned in several countries, largely on the grounds that they were an abomination unto the Lord rather than for the more obvious reason that they would

125

make you and the animal brown bread. Which is to say that when Dr William Thornton showed up at Washington's side too late to save him, he carried with him the idea that injecting humans with the blood of animals was a good idea. He suggested to the people mourning the death of the President that he should reanimate his corpse, already in rigor mortis, by pumping it full of lamb's blood. He then planned (why the hell not?) to warm the president with blankets, before performing a tracheotomy and inflating his lungs like a balloon, thus curing his condition of [checks medical textbook] being extremely fucking toast.

Fortunately for Washington, his family intervened and demanded that Thornton leave his body be, which was good news for his dignity, but very bad news for everyone who wonders what it would have been like to have an undead zombie sheep politician years before Boris Johnson came into office.

DOGS HAVE A SOMETIMES FATAL ATTRACTION TO MINK ANUS

There is a bridge in West Dunbartonshire, Scotland, that, legend (and a big tally of dog deaths) has it, is a suicide hotspot for dogs.

Since the 1950s, around fifty dogs have thrown themselves to their deaths off the Overtoun Bridge, with over six hundred doing the same but miraculously surviving the fall into the gorge below. Owners report that, in a certain spot towards one end of the bridge, the animals simply decide 'Right, that's enough living for me' and jump over the bridge wall, plunging to their deaths. Some that survive have even gone back for another crack at it. In a naming convention similar to Walky Talky and a child pointing at a fridge and saying 'food box', the bridge has been conveniently nicknamed 'the dog suicide bridge' for quite some time now. 'Something overcame Bonnie as soon as we approached the bridge,' one dog owner told the *New York Times*.[73] 'At first she froze, but then she became possessed by a strange energy and ran and jumped right off the parapet.'

You don't watch hundreds of dogs trying to dead themselves without coming up with a few creepy theories. People have put it down to either a ghost that haunts a nearby house that only dogs can see (why not add in the detail that she died holding a bag of Bonio to lure them in, if you're going to go this wacky); or that it's triggered by a hum that only dogs can hear from a nearby nuclear power station/some dick using a whistle – like a pied piper that's clearly going to get the shit kicked out of him by John Wick.

Before we move on to more realistic explanations, there have been similar claims of animals 'killing themselves' elsewhere, including the dolphin from *Flipper* who, according to its handler, just suffocated itself in front of him[74] (maybe after seeing a particularly bad review) and a herd of cows that ran off a cliff in Switzerland in 2009,[75] clearly trying to get away from all that fucking yodelling. However, animal behaviour experts and psychologists (and anyone who has seen a dog be surprised by the pain that biting its own tail causes) agree that animals lack the foresight and knowledge that what they are doing will kill themselves. Besides, dogs love life. You'd have to be eating the best meal you ever had, beating your Tetris high score and landing your dream job at the precise moment of climax to experience just a fraction of the pleasure that a dog feels when he sees a medium-sized stick. These dogs are not in any way intentionally trying to end things.

So, what's really going on? Well, one of the clues lies in the type of dogs that appear to be jumping off the bridge, which is mostly long-nosed breeds. The owner of the supposedly haunted manor overlooking the bridge suggested that the mink and pine martens beneath the bridge might be causing the dogs to jump off.

Mink produce a particularly pungent aroma. They have a weak sense of smell, but make up for it by having powerful anal glands, which they rub on the ground to mark their scent. When stressed, they expel the contents of their anal glands too, which is why you never find them at parties. The smell is supposedly worse than skunks, according to people who, in my opinion, have gone too much out of their way to smell ass. The dogs, actively enjoying the smell, may simply be catching a whiff and – especially on clear days, which is when the jumps reportedly happen the most – they leap in the smell's general direction. A TV show investigating the idea in 2010 found that dogs prefer the scent of mink over even that of a squirrel or a mouse, suggesting that they really, really do love the mink anus and are willing to do anything it takes to get a whiff. As for why they only risk their death on this bridge, animal behaviourist David Sands concluded in the documentary that the bridge's parapets are too tall for the dogs to see over and notice the drop on the other side.

So, good news dog owners, it's not that the dogs are depressed and suicidal, it's most likely that they are so overwhelmed with joy when they catch the smell of a mink's arsehole that they can't resist a fatal fall. Which is quite the compliment for mink.

ANDY, THE CELEBRITY GOOSE
WHO WORE SHOES

Andy the Goose

In 1988, 12-year-old Jessica Fleming arrived home at her parents' and grandparents' house in Nebraska when she saw her grandfather walking a goose with a leash. That's not really something you ignore; either something amazing had happened or Grandpa Gene was on track for an intervention. She approached and soon realised that the leash was the least of their problems, for the goose – named Andy, like geese often are, shut up – was wearing a pair of people trainers.

Her grandfather had found Andy on his sister-in-law's farm, and, upon seeing that the goose had no feet, decided to intervene. At first, as your mind would, Gene leapt to the idea of attaching a skateboard to one of the goose's stumps and letting it push itself around the farm like some sort of deranged mashup between Untitled Goose Game and Tony Hawk's Pro Skateboarding. The skateboard idea failed, because it was fucking insane. Gene moved on from this setback and instead put the goose in tiny baby shoes. Before he knew it, Andy the goose had mastered people shoes and was running around all over the place. Jessica, who was a tween and embarrassed about her family already, wasn't too happy that she now had to explain to her friends, 'Yes, we've got a goose with shoes on, don't ... don't look at it,' as it waddled its way into the room.

Not much happens in Hastings, Nebraska, I'm forced to assume, as news of the goose soon hit the front pages of the local press. At least I hope nothing happens in Hastings, Nebraska, as I'd hate to be the relative of someone who was murdered and was pushed back to page five by Andy the fucking human-shoed goose. Soon though, the goose cracked the whole of America, after the national papers picked up the story and ran with it. The goose appeared on Johnny Carson and went to Hollywood, which can't have felt great for actors and comedians watching some goose take their shot at the limelight. The goose became a sort of mascot for disabled children around America, and started negotiating sponsorship deals. He would wear shoes from different brands in exchange for money, selling out and forgetting his goose roots.

Then, on 19 October 1991, Gene received a call from a concerned friend, who had heard that a goose had been killed and dismembered in the town park. It wasn't clear at that point that it was Andy, but for one vital clue: NONE OF THE OTHER GEESE IN THE WORLD WORE SHOES.

Andy was missing, and the body was confirmed to be him. What's more, the family investigated the backyard where Andy had been caged, and found two sets of footprints. One set was the normal everyday goose footprints that you'd expect to find, but the other footprints were larger, clearly from a human, or perhaps a slightly larger goose. It was, forgive me Jesus, a murder most fowl. 'The instant we looked at his poor dismembered body, we knew it was him,' Gene told the *Chicago Tribune*,[76] not even considering the possibility that someone had rammed shoes onto a separate goose, or taking a moment to apologise to that day's shoe sponsor. 'Andy died with his boots on.'

Of course, a media storm descended on the town once more. Even though people probably ate goose, or at least usually couldn't give a shit if a goose died, they hated the idea that someone would do this to a goose that had made the effort to wear shoes. Reward money came flooding in for anybody with any information. Little tip: if your cat goes missing and nobody cares, tell them it likes to wear a tuxedo and you might be in business. Condolence cards came in absurd numbers, and a gravestone was paid for by fans, and tips for the murder investigation kept coming. The police followed up on a lot of the leads, but found nothing.

We'll never know exactly what happened to Andy, the celebrity goose that wore shoes. A well-planned murder, mistaken for people? Or maybe, just maybe, somebody saw a goose wearing people shoes and freaked the fuck out and tried to smash its brains in before we ended up in a Planet of the Apes situation, but with geese.

AUSTRALIA STARTED A WAR
WITH THE EMU AND LOST

In one of the most on-brand stories in Australian history, the Australian military once declared war on emus.

At the end of World War I, soldiers returned home to Australia. Many of them were struggling for work when they did, so the government hatched a plan. If there's one thing the country has in abundance, apart from an eerie feeling that at any time of day or night you're either going to be killed by a crocodile or a scary bastard who has fought crocodiles, it's a fuckload of land nobody wants. Probably because of the aforementioned crocodiles and scary bastards.

They settled upon a scheme to give veterans plots of land around the country to farm. Soon they ran out of good land and started buying up any old shit that resembled land but wouldn't grow a thing, which people, who were mainly good at shooting now, had to grow stuff out of. I suppose you could think of forking the earth as a bit like bayoneting a pudgy enemy combatant, but other than this I see very few transferable skills.

Even experienced farmers would have had trouble with the land, and though the veterans did their best, times were tough, and a decade later they would be a lot tougher. The Great Depression hit, and wheat prices plummeted. The government said they would subsidise wheat production, but you won't be shocked to hear that the caring administration that told a bunch of soldiers who'd just got back from the actual trenches to get digging didn't follow through on this.

Then there were the emus.

Emus were protected in Australia way up until 1922, despite the fact they're giant two-metre feathered demon birds that can more than look after themselves. They were reclassified as vermin due to their growing numbers and tendency to trash farms by eating the produce or running through the wheat like a 30 mph Theresa May. By 1932 there were over 20,000 of them going around the place destroying livelihoods. At least a lot of the Theresa Mays would have been distracted by trying to deport the camels.

The veterans were, as you'd expect, quite good at killing and, after the horrors of the Somme, probably not that squeamish about shooting a massive chicken. Yet still the emus kept coming. The farmers were wasting all their money on ammo, only not to kill enough emus to make even a dent, and every time they had been 'successful', they had a gigantic corpse to deal with. So, with pressure mounting, the Australian government decided to skip phases such as controlled culls or maybe even building some sort of fence, and decided to declare war on what I really must stress were some birds.

The military was sent in, led by Major G.P.W. Meredith of the Seventh Heavy Battery of the Royal Australian Artillery. Considering he was trained in heavy artillery to be used in real war, this would be like sending in Mike Tyson to fight some primary school green belt in judo. Or so you'd think. The first assault began with the army creeping up on the emus Elmer Fudd style and then opening fire when they were close enough. Having not expected the fucking military to creep up on them and open fire with actual machine guns while they were eating a nice bit of dinner, the emus scattered, making it more difficult for the army.

The emus were quick learners. A lot faster, in fact, than the military. According to reports at the time, the birds 'soon began to improve their own understanding of the science of warfare'.[77] 'The emus have proved that they are not so stupid as they are usually considered to be,' one of the army recruits informed the media at

136

the time,[78] not realising it was hardly a massive PR win to tell the papers how you were being outsmarted by a bird. 'Each mob has its leader, always an enormous black-plumed bird standing fully six-feet high, who keeps watch while his fellows busy themselves with the wheat. At the first suspicious sign, he gives the signal, and dozens of heads stretch up out of the crop. A few birds will take fright, starting a headlong stampede for the scrub, the leader always remaining until his followers have reached safety.'

Everything the humans tried failed, and they tried some real *Apocalypse Now* shit, including mounting a machine gun on a truck and trying to mow the emus down on the move. They soon found they were unable to aim while doing this, and one of the few emus that they did hit with bullets ended up getting caught up in the truck, causing it to veer wildly and smash into a farmer's fence.

The war, though casualties only occurred on the emu side, was one of attrition. The Australian army kept trying, and each time they went out there they killed very few emus. Eventually, the government realised they were spending a *lot* of money on ammunition for very few kills, expending about ten bullets per hit. The military admitted defeat and withdrew the troops, the only army to have lost a war to an animal later described in a scientific journal as the dumbest bird alive.[79]

THE POLICE SPENT MANY YEARS CHASING A SERIAL KILLER THAT DIDN'T FUCKING EXIST

Between the years of 1993 and 2009, police in Heilbronn, Germany, tracked down just about the most elusive serial killer since Ted Cruz. Known as the Phantom of Heilbronn, or occasionally The Woman Without A Face, she was implicated in so many crimes that the police eventually put out a reward of €300,000 for any information leading to her arrest.[80]

The case that brought her to the media's attention and earned her two ridiculously badass nicknames (honestly, if you don't want people to commit murders you're going to have to come up with less glamorous nicknames – what's wrong with Jack Shitshispants or the Zodiac Cuck?) took place in April 2007. Twenty-two-year-old police officer Michèle Kiesewetter and her partner were taking a lunch break when two unseen assailants climbed in the back of their car and shot both of them from behind, killing Kiesewetter and injuring her colleague. Nobody got a good look at the killers, and there was basically no evidence to go on – but for a tiny microscopic bit of DNA found on the dashboard and the back seat of the BMW. When they ran the DNA, it opened up one of the biggest investigations in German history, spanning fifteen years.

The DNA – that of a woman – didn't just match one crime scene, it matched all over the place. She appeared to be everywhere, killing folk or robbing some chump while spraying her DNA about, rubbing herself against evidence in the way Baloo rubs his ass on a tree.

As well as scenes of theft across three countries, the Phantom's DNA was found at scenes of brutal murders, with no obvious MO or theme. No calling card, like that of a serial killer who only kills at twilight or a mugger who always leaves a mug. Her DNA was found on a teacup at the brutal strangulation of a 62-year-old woman in May 1993 in Idar-Oberstein, on a car that had been used to ferry the bodies of three Georgians killed in January 2008 in Heppenheim, on a heroin needle in October 2001 near Gerolstein. You name it, there she was, spraying her DNA all over the crime scene like spray tan onto a contestant on *The Only Way Is Essex*.

Then there were some insane curveballs to throw into the evidence box labelled 'What the fuck is going on?' Her DNA showed up on a toy pistol that was involved in a robbery, and was found at several other crime scenes that involved accomplices. None of those interviewed ever said they were with a woman, which the police put down to them being too terrified or loyal to talk.[81]

There was no real pattern to any of it. This woman was apparently tearing across the country, committing crimes of desperation while throwing a few mob hits into the mix. Despite the DNA declaring she was a woman, scant witness reports sometimes described her as a man, adding to the confusion. In 2005, two brothers started a domestic dispute and one brother fired on the other, *and then the police found her DNA on the bullet*. She was either the most elusive serial killer of the century, or . . . she didn't exist.

In 2009, a new piece of evidence showed up: a burned cadaver found in France, which was thought to be the body of an asylum seeker who had disappeared seven years earlier. The police checked the fingerprints on the man's application and found – drumroll please – the Phantom's DNA. 'Obviously that was impossible, as the asylum seeker was a man and the Phantom's DNA belonged to a woman,' a spokesman for the Saarbrücken public prosecutor's office told *Der Spiegel*.

Somewhat weirded out, they checked again. This time there was no match. All of a sudden, fifteen years of evidence crumbled into dust, was bagged and labelled 'not fucking evidence'.

What had happened was that during the manufacturing process of the swabs used to take DNA, some hapless employee at the swab factory had contaminated all the swabs. Cotton swabs are sterilised prior to being used in a crime scene, but just occasionally DNA can survive the process, at which point it was put *onto* crime scenes all over the place.

They had been tracking their own swabs, like Scooby fucking Doo following his own footprints in the snow.

THE BYFORD DOLPHIN
DIVING BELL ACCIDENT

On 5 November 1983, an accident happened on an oil rig that makes merely drowning to death (which also happened at the same oil rig) seem like quite a nice thing to do with your time. On the Norwegian rig the Byford Dolphin (a name that makes you feel like, at worst, you're going to a depressing rip-off of Seaworld), four divers were going about their usual day, probably remarking on how great it was not to get sucked through a 24-inch hole before having their giblets sprayed across the rig, when events took a turn for the giblet thing.

Several people were working in the diving bell that day, a rigid chamber that can take you to unholy depths no human is meant to reach. As they go underwater, the people inside the chamber are put under immense physical pressure from the water surrounding them. The air is highly compressed, meaning the internal pressure too can be extremely high.

As you'd imagine, when you're under high pressure you can't just open the door to a low-pressure atmosphere and expect to go on living. I know you're probably picturing being shot out of the diving bell like a champagne cork, and though it's similar to that if the cork was made of mincemeat, it's oh so much worse. To prevent this from happening, the usual procedure on this particular rig was for two divers outside to make sure the diving bell could be attached to a series of decompression chambers and passageways at a lower pressure than inside the bell, so the pressure could be gradually decreased to the point that the divers inside the bell could open the door without exploding.

On this day, things went wrong. The divers had crawled out of the diving bell, as per usual, and had made their way up the tube into compression chamber 1 above them. The door to the diving bell had been sealed, and now they would usually depressurise. Slowly. Once that was achieved, the divers would close the door to the trunk that connected to the diving bell, which would then be safely detached. Meanwhile, in a separate chamber connected to decompression chamber 1, two other divers would be waiting, ready to open the doors once their pressures matched.

For some reason that we'll never know because of what was about to happen, one of the attendants outside the diving bell decided to open the clamp before he should have done, maybe hoping to clock off early. Which, in a manner of speaking, he did. Opening the clamp meant that the chamber system, which was under nine atmospheres of pressure, was now connected to the outside with its usual one atmosphere of pressure. The diving bell shot away with tremendous force, instantly killing the person who would otherwise have been asked 'Now why the hell did you do that?'

Being bludgeoned to death by a diving bell, in these circumstances, was a bit vanilla. Three of the four divers in the compression chambers were likely killed instantly as the fluids inside their bodies – yes, all of them, even the sex ones – expanded with incredible speed, rupturing all the bits inside them they needed to live and causing haemorrhages all over the place. In their last few seconds alive, their blood boiled and essentially melted their surrounding fat, which leaked out of their bodies and turned them into a kind of fat-free crouton in a surprisingly fatty soup.

The fourth diver was sent to the autopsy in four separate bags, collected from various different locations around the rig, with one miscellaneous body part collected from ten metres above the chambers.[82] Every part of the body inside these bags of mystery meat showed some sign of injury.

Diver number four had been closest to the opening that was created when the clamp was released, and as such he had the honour of being sucked out of a hole just twenty-four inches across. The autopsy, which I didn't realise at first had images but will now be forever sealed into my brain, revealed that 'the soft tissues of the face were found', which is the most nightmarish sentence I'd read until I came across the next part: 'completely separated from the bones'. Many pieces of the man were missing, or else were completely shattered and destroyed. His penis, though present, was 'invaginated', meaning it had been sucked back into his body like a belly button. Which, I suppose, was the least of his worries.

NOT ALL DOGS GO TO HEAVEN

In 1908 Paris, there lived a dog that became a 'who's a good boy, who's a good boy', before becoming a 'bad dog, BAD DOG'. Sorry to talk like this, but it's very important that your dog learns the following behaviour is unacceptable.

In a story so damning it could have been written by a cat, the *New York Times* tells the tale of a Newfoundland dog that once heard a boy screaming for help in the Seine. With no regard for its own health, probably because dogs have no concept of death – as we learnt back on page 129, a mink's a-hole is more important than safety any day – the dog shot off in search of the screaming, and leapt into the river.

The dog saved the life of the child and was rightly praised. The father also gave the dog a big slab of beef as payment for his services, which rather makes you think how much he severely undervalued his kid. I have no idea how damaging it must have been for a child to learn their father valued their life about as much as the shit part of a Sunday roast. If you don't know roasts are all about the potatoes I don't know how to help you.

Massive psychological damage aside, all was well. The kid was safe and the dog full of beef. A few days later, however, another kid was playing by the Seine when they too fell into the water. Hero dog, having digested his beef to the point that he was buoyant again, dived in once more and rescued the child. Again, the dog was rewarded with some meat. I should mention at this point that I realise that dogs want very few things and it would be useless to get it an Xbox, but at the same time there's a big difference between that and just giving it food.

This weird pattern of near child-drownings and dog rescue went on for quite some time before the parents really showed an interest. They thought maybe someone was pushing the kids in the river, for reasons unknown.

Of course, if they'd stopped to think for even a second they'd have realised that only the dog, now 90 per cent beef, had a motive to keep drowning kids. It was an inside job. According to the *New York Times*, 'whenever he saw a playing child on the edge of the stream he promptly knocked it into the water',[83] before rescuing the child and then waiting around for some beef. It was like Pavlov's dog, but instead of salivating whenever it heard a bell, humans would give it some filet mignon every time it endangered the life of a toddler.

A FACT CHECK OF
BONEY M'S 'RASPUTIN'

Some of you might have heard the story of Rasputin's death, being as he's one of the few people in history to have a song written about their assassination. There aren't many people out there whose deaths are an absolute tune. For those of you who aren't into the oeuvre of Boney M, let's recap the tale, as well as fill in some of the details that Boney couldn't be arsed to include. If there's one thing he's known for, it's choosing rhyme structure over proper historical context.

Grigori Rasputin was born a peasant in a village in Siberia. He grew up, married another villager and had children, before spending months in a monastery in 1897 where he underwent a religious conversion, setting in train a series of events that would lead to him becoming one of the most influential – and horniest – monks on record. Rasputin moved shortly afterwards to St Petersburg, where the church couldn't get enough of him. He wasn't actually an official monk, having failed to abandon his former life, including his wife and children, but he soon made friends in high places at the church, maybe through his unkempt beard or 'I'm going to fucking kill you' eyes.

In November 1905, he had the chance to meet with Emperor

Nicholas and Empress Alexandra. He charmed them too, and became a faith healer to their haemophiliac son. On several occasions, he's said to have 'healed' the boy following various haematomas. Historians speculate that this could have been because of his unwillingness to let doctors go near the boy, thus preventing the child from being given aspirin (which thins the blood and would have added to clotting bleeding problems, something they didn't realise at the time).

Rasputin earned a lot of favour with the court, which is nineteenth-century talk for they found him dope, which in turn is 30-year-old dad speak for 'they liked him a lot'. He became a powerful advisor to the royal family and immediately used this power and influence to gain sexual favours, being one of those monks that are mainly in it for the pussy.

His behaviour and influence with Alexandra soon earned him a reputation with the public, and he became the subject of many escalating rumours and scandals. During World War I, soldiers believed that he and Alexandra were having an affair (Mr M would go on to repeat this claim in the line 'rah rah Rasputin, lover of the Russian Queen', again sacrificing the historical accuracy of her position for the rhyme, the fucking charlatan), before stories started to spread that he was committing treason with Germany, and that he had poisoned a bunch of apples in St Petersburg in order to start a cholera epidemic.[84] Despite the banger that was clearly coming decades after his death, people didn't like the 'mad monk' and wanted him to be more of a 'dead monk'.

Here's where we get to the bit that would turn him from just some horndog monk into the stuff of legend. On 30 December 1916, aristocrat Prince Felix Felixovich Yusupov invited Rasputin over to the Moika Palace. There he was meant to have poisoned Rasputin's wine and cakes with cyanide. According to these accounts, Rasputin just drank the wine, asked for a few more glasses, ate the cakes and got up without even remarking that they tasted a bit like he might die. Sensing the job was not done, Felix is said to have shot Rasputin several times through the heart. He and some co-conspirators then took his body back to Rasputin's pad in order to make it look like he'd returned home that night. This is when Rasputin jumped back to life and chased him to the palace courtyard, where Rasputin was shot and twatted with heavy objects until he was co-operative enough to get inside some carpet and be dropped in a river. Which is to say, he was dead. 'This devil who was dying of poison, who had a bullet in his heart, must have been raised from the dead by the powers of evil,' read one account. 'There was something appalling and monstrous in his diabolical refusal to die.' According to rumours, he wasn't even dead when he went in the river, and had actually drowned.

For some reason, this story really took hold in people's minds, and has become *the* version of events. I can only speculate that people find it really badass when people drown. But this version of events is . . . the account of the murderer.

Following the investigation of Rasputin's murder, one of the conspirators was sent by Alexandra to the Western Front, whereas, as is fitting for a gentleman murderer, Felix was banished to one of his smaller but still unnecessarily massive properties. Here he wrote memoirs of that time he murdered a horny monk, not even bothering to cleverly title it '*IF* I murdered that horny monk' to cover his own back. His account was extremely exaggerated, and designed to make *him* look a lot more badass than he really was. In reality, Rasputin hadn't necked a bunch of poison, asked for more poison before refusing to die, and revived himself, he'd merely been invited to a place before being shot through the head immediately.

There was no evidence that he'd been poisoned, and his lungs were water free. The man who Felix had hired to poison the cake and wine later confessed on his deathbed that he had backed away from the idea at the last moment, meaning the only thing Rasputin had survived that night was a bit of wine and an ordinary cake. The legend of Rasputin who refused to die did so in the same way that Paul Hollywood refuses to die after sampling a *Great British Bake Off* contestant's flan.

So I guess the thing you don't want to know in this chapter is Rasputin isn't a badass, you can't trust the testimony of a murderer, and nobody is fucking fact-checking any of Boney M's songs.

A PILOT HAD TO LAND A PASSENGER PLANE WITH HIS COLLEAGUE HANGING OUT THE WINDOW

In 1990, most of a pilot was sucked out of the window of an aeroplane, leaving just enough pilot inside the plane for a steward to hold on to (specifically, the leg part). Then, the other pilot attempted to land the plane, probably while being quite distracted by all of the air and colleague that was flying out of the window.

On 10 June 1990, British Airways Flight 5390 was due to depart from Birmingham Airport, England, for Málaga Airport in Spain. The pilots followed the usual procedures and were at about 17,300 feet when passengers heard a loud 'bang', which is way up there with 'What does this button do?' and 'Oh fuck, I really shouldn't have pressed that button' in the top ten of sounds you don't want to hear coming from a cockpit. Unbeknown to the pilots, who had loosened their belts and shoulder harnesses for comfort, a maintenance manager had carried out a bit of work on the plane that would result in a quite ridiculous disaster.

The aircraft had needed its cockpit windows replacing, so a few nights prior to take-off, a mechanic had decided to give it a go. This was in spite of the fact he hadn't changed a windscreen in about two years. According to the Air Accidents Investigations Branch official report into the incident,[85] he briefly glanced at the maintenance manual, wanting to 'refresh his memory', like a surgeon going, 'Bit out of practice on the old surgery, might brush up a bit by slicing open somebody's brain.'

When selecting the bolts to replace the window, you might think that he'd be extra careful to select the correct ones, given that he was rustier than the screws he took out. But that is the opinion of a boring fucking nerd. The mechanic (who is much, much cooler than you) found the correct bolts by comparing the old bolts to the new ones he found in the screw drawers, like your

153

dad would, probably muttering 'Fuck it, that'll do' at the same time. This was in the middle of the night, around 3 a.m., meaning he'd have to compare the bolts by sight in the dark rather than read the labels. (Yes, that's right. There were labels he could have read, you fucking Melvin, you gigantic fucking Dwayne.)

The result was that many of the bolts he actually fitted to the plane were one size too small, and not enough to hold the windscreen together at high altitude. I guess this is why, famously, when you're performing repairs on an aircraft, you'd usually use some sort of fucking torch.

Back in the cockpit a few days later, Captain Tim Lancaster was about to learn this lesson the hard way. The 'bang' was the sound of the port window panel flying away from the aircraft. Lancaster, propelled by the sudden decompression, shot towards the window. Fortunately, from a him-not-dying point of view, his knees became stuck on the console. Unfortunately, from an everyone-else-not-dying perspective, his knees became stuck on the console, which is famously used to keep the plane away from the ground.

The number three steward, who was hopefully promoted to number one steward after this, rushed in and grabbed him by the waist and held on tight. The other stewards kept their cool, secured all the other loose items and somehow told the passengers everything was going to be OK while keeping a straight face. The guy who was really keeping it cool though was Lancaster, who was hanging out the window of an aircraft and being exposed to the extreme cold. Everyone inside the plane adopted their brace positions, other than Lancaster – who really should have been disciplined for choosing instead to assume the position of a wacky inflatable arm-flailing tube man on the outside of the aircraft, the maverick.

The situation inside the aircraft was even worse than Lancaster, the man hanging out of the aircraft, knew. The autopilot had disengaged, meaning they were now descending rapidly, and the flight deck door had been blown inwards onto the control panel, causing the plane to accelerate as it descended. Don't want to get too technical on you, but in the aviation world accelerating towards the ground is what's known as 'bad'.

The co-pilot regained control of the plane, while other crew members entered the cockpit and attempted to yank Lancaster back in like a yo-yo, rather than a human experiencing the kind of wind speeds that would make even Dorothy and Toto shit themselves. They sort of presumed he was dead already, but couldn't risk his corpse getting sucked into the jet engine and jamming it up like ten years' worth of hair in Robin Williams's plug hole. Worse was still to come. As the steward holding the captain became tired and frostbitten – enduring temperatures of around minus 21 Celsius plus wind chill – an exchange was required with another crew member (passing Lancaster like a fragile baton), and he slipped another six to eight inches out of the window in the handover.

With no way to pull him in, given the forces involved, the co-pilot was forced to land with his pilot hanging out of the window, being held onto by his ankles. Which sounds a tad distracting if I'm honest, and the co-pilot demonstrated enormous restraint by not shouting 'Would you mind cutting out this-hanging-out-of-the-window shit, I'm trying to land a fucking Boeing 747 here.'

Astonishingly, the landing was successful, and no passengers were harmed in this trip that would be later rejected as a prequel to *Airplane* for being too unbelievable. The only injuries sustained were to the steward, who had mild bruising and frostbite, and the pilot, who had bone fractures in his right arm and wrist, a broken left thumb, bruising, frostbite and – surprise surprise – shock.

THE FRENCH ACCIDENTALLY PAID A LOT OF MONEY FOR MASS RAT-MAIMING

In Hanoi, Vietnam, rats were a huge problem around the turn of the twentieth century. Or to be more blunt about things, they had been a massive problem for years, but the colonial French had also begun viewing them as a problem when they realised it affected them too.

Alexandre Yersin had discovered the bacillus bacteria responsible for the bubonic plague, and now everyone knew that rats and fleas spread it. Since rats would occasionally use the pipes that served the flushing toilets of the colonials (unavailable to the local population, of course) as an entry point into their homes, suddenly the pests, largely kept away from the colonials' spacious mansions and confined to the poorer Vietnamese areas of Hanoi, moved from being 'no biggie' to 'they must be destroyed this fucking instant'. It's funny how a problem suddenly becomes a problem that needs to be dealt with when it affects colonists, especially when that problem pokes its head out of the shitter.

Now worried about the plague and concerned for the city that they'd taken by force, the French got to work and dealt with the problem by themselves. I am of course fucking with you: they hired locals to travel down into the cramped, dank sewers in order to kill the potentially disease-filled rats below, for a pittance. While you'd probably think giving money to random people who are up for a bit of rat twatting is bound to have some problems down the line, the administration (who you'll soon find out lacked a lot of foresight) wasn't worried about training the people they were subjugating how to kill.

The rat killers were pretty good for first timers, and in the first week of the project they managed to kill 7,985 rats.[86] An absolute bloodbath, I'm sure you'll agree in an awed tone. As their techniques improved (sadly we have no records of how they improved, so you're going to have to picture a montage of killers taking out rats with a series of ever larger lawnmowers) they managed to kill as many as 20,114 rats in a single day. Which, even as someone who's not a fan of old rat torture, I have to grudgingly admit is quite impressive. Somebody says, 'I twatted this rat to death,' I'm the first to move seats on the bus, but say 'I killed 20,000 rats' and I'm clapping and asking how.

Despite what can only be described as rat carnage and the death of many potential Ratatouilles, it soon became obvious that they weren't even putting a tiny dent in the rat population. The colonial administration began to pay even more amateur vigilantes to kill rats. Or so they thought.

Deciding that it would be too much of an effort to deal in rat corpses, even before you consider the smell and plague possibilities, the colonial rulers decided that they would pay one cent per rat tail, rather than for the whole rat. At first the scheme looked like a massive success, if you define success as 'a big pile of rat tails began flooding in', which I do not but I'm not going to kink-shame you in a book.

It looked like people were slaughtering the rodents in impressive numbers. Soon, though, officials venturing into the Vietnamese part of the city took a closer look at some of the rats running around and noticed a distinct lack of tail where the tail should be. Rather than killing the rats, entrepreneurial types had merely cut off their rat tails and released them into the wild, to breed more valuable rat tails. Essentially, in an attempt to incentivise rat killing, the government had accidentally incentivised rat maiming, pretty much in the same way that the British accidentally incentivised breeding cobras in India by paying for dead cobras.

Worse, people started farming the rats themselves in order to make money. The rat population exploded, and a year later the city began to see cases of bubonic plague, followed by a larger outbreak in 1906. Sweet revenge for the rats.

DUMB WORLD RECORDS

Sooner or later, all of the best records have been set to such a standard that nobody but an absolute superhero or someone pumped full of just the right amount of steroids could ever hope to come close to breaking one. You'd have to be either Usain Bolt's younger drug-filled brother or a bit thick to think you could take on Usain Bolt's 100m record, for instance. This pretty much leaves you with the option of either giving up on the dream of being best in the world at something, or thinking up a record so unfeasibly stupid no other person would ever bother to try:

Recipient of the world's hardest kick in the dick

'Hey ma, I made it.'

'What did you do?'

'I'm a record breaker, ma –'

'In?'

'Don't worry about it.'

'Why do you sound like you've just been kicked in the dick, Timmy?'

Roy Kirby is a man who looks like an ordinary bank manager. You'd never suspect that this guy has been kicked in the dick harder than anybody on the planet that we know of. He set the record for being kicked in the peen live on Fox Sports News, after the channel hired an MMA fighter to do the honours.[87]

The MMA fighter kicked Kirby in the penis and nuts at 22 mph – imagine a car coming right at you, but it only hits your dick – with 1100 lb of force. Though he was kicked so hard his feet physically left the ground, he only let out the kind of shriek you'd make if you'd stubbed your toe on the door. The programme explained that, despite being fairly likeable in appearance, he had been kicked in the balls so many times over the years he only produced about 10 per cent of the neurotransmitter a normal person would under the same circumstances. In pursuit of his frankly insane goal, his balls had become jaded.

A man who ate a plane
Before Michel Lotito died, he ate bicycles, a computer, a bed, a coffin, a pair of skis and a light aircraft. Amazingly, none of these were the cause of death.

Lotito had a condition known as pica, which is a disorder where you develop an appetite for things that aren't food. It can cause horrible knock-on effects, with people swallowing everything from human hair to hundreds of nails and needles.[88] A showman, Lotito turned his condition into an act. He would eat inedible things – which to him were just lunch – in front of paying audiences, which you have to admit is one hell of a business model. Nobody has so far offered to pay me to eat cheese.

The lining of his stomach was incredibly thick, which came in handy when it came to eating an entire plane. The task took him two years, eating the plane in small chunks over that time, while still snacking on other metals, plastic and wood. He remains to this day the only man to have ever shat out a light aircraft.

Most snails on face
An 11-year-old won the record for having the largest number of live snails crawling around on his face.[89] The forty-three snails, placed there by family and friends who really should have been asking him if there was anything going on at school they should talk about, remained on his face for a full ten seconds, unaware of their part in history. The boy's dreams – like having a face underneath forty-three snails – were shat on pretty hard after that,

however, when the *Guinness Book of Records* decided this was too dumb for even them to include.

Most balloons released

All the other dumb records pale in comparison to balloonfest 86, in which the charity United Way of Cleveland, Ohio, decided to release 1.5 million helium balloons.[90] They hadn't really thought it through, and as a cold front came in the balloons were pushed down towards the ground, where they caused mayhem and several deaths. Cars swerved out of the way of the balloons, causing traffic accidents. A group of prize horses got spooked – horses don't even know what a birthday balloon is, how the hell were they supposed to contextualise this – and allegedly injured themselves horrifically. An airport had to close.

Worst of all, two fishermen had gone missing on Lake Erie the day before the event, and helicopters looking for them were forced to call off the search after the balloons interfered with their vision. The men's bodies were later found, washed ashore like the millions of balloons that preceded them.

THE TWO-HEADED FRANKEN-DOGS

Every now and then, humans are curious about what would happen if something didn't have a head (as you'll see in the next story), or if it had two heads, or some number of heads that's slightly above or below the average number of heads.

Enter Frankenpupper.

You look at a dog, I look at a dog, and very rarely will the thought 'I reckon that could do with another head' cross your mind, but you aren't Vladimir Demikhov. Now sometimes the word 'pioneer' is used in a positive way, as in the sentence 'Elon Musk is a pioneer, look how he sends new rockets to space.' Occasionally it's not so good, as in the sentence 'Elon Musk is a pioneer, first major CEO to call a rescue worker a "pedo guy" on Twitter.' Demikhov, born in Russia in 1918, was both of these things. He performed heart transplants in animals that paved the way for human heart transplants today, and carried out the first coronary artery bypass on a mammal.[91] But people tend not to remember that sort of thing when you also take the head off a dog and put it on a second, unsuspecting dog.

His experiments started modestly, gradually becoming more and more grim as they went. In the way that you might enjoy baking brownies before moving on to a flan, Demikhov began by removing the organs of dogs to see which ones they could live without, before having a crack at turning one dog into 1.5 dogs. On 24 February 1954, Demikhov began the experiments that would change his place in history from 'Hey, isn't that the guy that pioneered the operation that saved Grandpa?' to 'Hey, isn't that the arsehole that mutilated dogs for kicks?'

He cut off most of the front half of a puppy and attached it to the back half of a larger dog.[92] You won't be surprised to learn that the first few dogs he tried this on didn't last very long. Despite being one of the few people in history who should have been told as a child, 'If at first you don't succeed, fucking stop,' he kept at it for [checks sources] *five fucking years (?!)* and eventually managed to keep one dog (or, if you prefer, two dogs) alive for twenty-nine nightmarish days of existence, each day an abomination unto the dog Lord, before they were granted the sweet release of death. The puppy on top was able to move its own front legs independently of the dog below. Not having a stomach, it didn't need food. But when it drank, the water would spill out of its severed neck onto the donor dog's spine, which must have been the most disconcerting thing that happened to it since it fell asleep one day and when it woke up it felt heavier and its friend Jeff had gone.

'The big dog', meanwhile, 'doesn't understand,' Demikhov said, in what would go on to be the creepiest defence of all time.[93] 'He feels some kind of inconvenience, but he doesn't know what it is. Sometimes the puppy will playfully bite the ear of the big dog and Pirat will shake his head but he never has tried to scratch or kick off the extra head.' It's fine, everybody, it's not like the dog tried to kick its second head off. Quit your fucking whining, PETA.

Though Demikhov was, without a doubt, a man who should

have been banned from buying a suspicious amount of dogs, you could argue that what he did advanced medical science, and in rebuttal I'd call you a dog-hating probable cat fan. But so much worse was South African doctor Christiaan Barnard, who read about the dog head experiment in 1962. He decided to do it for himself that very afternoon in his hospital, remarking, 'Anything those Russians can do, we can do, too,' in a way that would have been acceptable if you were talking about knitting or making a nice pie but not hacking off dogs' heads, especially not in a normal hospital with human patients who needed medical attention. The dog lived for two days, which was just long enough for everybody to see the full horror of what he'd done but not long enough for them to think he was some sort of dog-sculpting genius.

Despite protests from medical students and animal rights activists, Barnard was able to shake the incident from his reputation, and went on to perform the first ever human heart transplant five years later.

Meanwhile, the spiritual successor to Demikhov, neurosurgeon Robert J. White, wasn't able to shake his reputation as the head guy, after he severed the spines of monkeys and replaced their heads with the heads of a second monkey, creating one dead monkey with a dead head and one paralysed second monkey. Not letting this astonishing success go to his own head, he went on to practise human head transplants on corpses in the morgue. He talked about performing the operation on Stephen Hawking,[94] though my guess is Hawking – one of the smartest people to ever live – knew better than to trust a guy who said 'Let me take your head off, I'm good at it,' before pointing at a pile of dead monkeys as proof.

THE NO-HEADED CHICKEN

Let's stay on the theme of things with the wrong number of heads, shall we?

Mike had survived World War II, largely by being a chicken. To clarify, I'm not a frothing right-wing war-era arsehole using a book on light trivia to randomly take a massive shit on conscientious objectors; he actually was a chicken. However, a few short weeks after the war ended, disaster struck. On 10 September 1945, farmers Lloyd and Clara Olson were beheading chickens together in Fruita, Colorado. Don't judge them, we all have to keep that spark alive somehow. A lot of people try beheading live animals and watching the blood spurt out the neck hole, though some people prefer candlelit baths. Everything was going swimmingly, from the perspective of anybody who wasn't a chicken, when Lloyd took an axe to one of the birds. Having had its head chopped off, it proceeded to run around flapping like, well, you know, some sort of headless dickhead.

This isn't actually all that unusual. I mean, it is unusual if you happen not to be in the game of ripping off chicken heads for a living, but it's not unheard of if that's how you spend your career or your free time. When you axe off a chicken's head, the pressure can trigger nerve endings in the neck, causing a final bit of energy to head down to the muscles and tell the chicken to fucking peg it.[95] The result is the chicken flaps and runs around while you, a seasoned chicken murderer, move on to the next batch.

However, what *was* unusual was that this particular rooster (HEY MA, I DIDN'T GO FOR A COCK JOKE, AM I A GROWNED UP OR WHAT) refused entirely to die.[96] The farmers placed the chicken in an old apple box, probably figuring the situation might just resolve itself, but when they got up the next morning there the chicken was, dicking around in the apple box. The chicken was still alive, even though it was missing its noodle.

At this point I'd like to say no offence, chickens, but it doesn't say great things about your species if your head isn't entirely necessary. No wonder your nan always offers you chicken when you've told her you're vegetarian; in terms of brain power, at best chickens are a fruit. Oh, I can hear you hypocrites out there saying chickens are smart, but when was the last time you went to one of them for mortgage advice? Hmmm? Didn't think so.

When Lloyd saw the grotesque and pitiful sight, he immediately thought, 'I could make a few quid here,' and headed into town with the chicken. You may think this was a cruel thing to do to an animal that clearly needed, at the very least, bed rest. But we should remember that it didn't care at all, largely because it didn't have a goddamn head.

Once in town, he began betting with people that he had a headless chicken out in his wagon, earning himself a bit of money and a few beers. Realising the bigger potential, he took the chicken on tour, joining the freak circuit where it became known as Mike the headless chicken. (Not the main thing, but it probably doesn't sit well with chickens that they're only rewarded with a name when they've received a baffling head injury.) To keep Mike alive, they would feed him grains, milk and other liquids with an eye dropper, directly into the hole at the top of his neck. They would also clear out any mucus that was in there using a syringe, to stop him from choking to death, turning him from a cash cow into nuggets.

Before Mike (completely unaware of everything that was going on) embarked on his tour, Lloyd took him to be studied by scientists at the University of Utah. Science operated more like a

mad hungry fox back then and, rumour has it, the university began ripping off the heads of other chickens to see if the same thing
would happen. What they hadn't clocked yet was that, though
Lloyd had ripped off most of Mike's head, he had missed a bit of
the brain, which was still functional in Mike's neck.

The farmers earned a fair amount of money off that one
chicken until one day, while on tour, they forgot their mucus syringe and Mike drowned in his own snot, a whopping eighteen
months after he'd stopped being in possession of a head. Lloyd's
great-grandson Troy thinks Lloyd probably tried to create a new
Mike by continuing to chop the heads off a little too high, like a
chicken Frankenstein.

DROWNING IN SUGAR AND BEER ISN'T AS MUCH FUN AS IT SOUNDS

I n terms of deaths, the thought of being killed by syrup or beer ranks just below being cuddled to death or fatally mauled by puppies. But in reality, they involve a lot more 'dying a horrible death' than you'd like. Let me explain.

The molasses flood

On 15 January 1919, people on the streets of Boston's North End were minding their own business when they heard a 'deep rumble',[97] which is up there with a narrator saying 'unbeknownst to Carl, this would be the day he shat himself to death' in terms of ominous sounds you don't want to ignore. A 50ft-tall steel tank of molasses had ruptured, causing 2.3 million gallons of one of the worst syrups known to humankind (honestly, how do you make something that's basically diabetes juice taste bad?) to flood through the streets like The Blob. The 160ft-wide wave of treacle reached 15 feet in height, and moved at an astonishing 35 mph – which was especially impressive back then, when cars would disintegrate if you tried to push them into second gear.

It was the perfect storm. There was clearly a massive threat to life, but if you were to try and warn someone by shouting 'LYLE'S GOLDEN SYRUP' it would probably only slow people down, as they paused to try and figure out what the hell you were talking about; did somebody bring a cake?

The wave destroyed part of the elevated railway and threw trains off the tracks, knocked whole buildings over and brought down electrical poles,[98] throwing into the mix the possibility of being electrocuted to death, like the world's deadliest flapjack. The syrup caused twenty-three deaths by the time it was over, and around $100 million worth of damage. Survivors and rescue workers on the scene found the dead covered in the stuff, which had filled their mouths and noses. The ones that couldn't be removed for days were encased in the syrup, like overgrown jelly babies, many beyond all recognition.

The cold caused the syrup to set, making rescue even more difficult. It was now so thick it was difficult to wade through, and occasionally needed to be chiselled. Police were forced to shoot the horses at a stables as the animals were stuck in the goo. One survivor who managed to cling to a ladder during the flood had to watch as a nearby horse drowned. On the bright side, the sugar gave them all an old-timey swear of 'Sugar!' to exclaim shortly before they perished, which now that I think about it was probably of little consolation.

The beer flood

On Monday 17 October 1814, the thing that many people only dream of occurred on the streets of London. Due to a fermentation tank bursting at the Horse Shoe Brewery on Tottenham Court Road, around 320,000 gallons of brown porter ale were released, causing a wave of alcohol 15 feet high to flood through the streets.[99]

As awesome as that sounds, the deaths began to mount up pretty quickly. In a nearby street, Mary Banfield and her daughter Hannah were drinking tea when, like a teetotaller at a stag do attempting to order a tonic water, a deadly amount of beer was forced upon them. They were both killed. Next, a family gathered in a basement of a nearby house for the wake of a two-year-old boy who had died the day before also fell victim. While they were probably remarking, 'How could this day get any worse?' the room flooded with beer, killing every one of the mourners. I'm far too respectful to make a joke about them drowning their sorrows here, so you're going to have to do that in your own head while I judge the shit out of you.

In total the flood killed eight victims on the day, though there are later reports claiming that a ninth died a week later, having been one of many to begin chugging at the scene of the disaster, necking pint after pint of death juice until they got sick from alcohol poisoning and died. The beer was hot and made dirty by the streets, but as is noted around the world, the English are fucking hooligans who like nothing better than a hot frothy beer on a warm summer's day, so maybe the rumours had merit.

THE LAWYER WHO LIKED
TO RUN AT WINDOWS

Garry Hoy was a lawyer at a firm in Toronto with an unusual patter for showing the new guys around. Whereas you might say 'There's the tea station' or, if you're Jeff Bezos, 'Don't even think about taking a piss break or it'll come up in your review,' Garry would run full pelt at the windows to show that they wouldn't break.[100]

Nobody knows why he developed this quirk, or why none of his co-workers asked him 'What the fuck are you playing at, the clients don't want to see their lawyers hurling themselves into a window, halfway through a meeting like a fucking crow. It doesn't scream "this firm's definitely capable of arguing my sentence down to manslaughter".' But have the quirk he did, and when new people came to look around the office it became an ordinary sight to see the 38-year-old charging top speed at the 24th-floor window.

Hoy was showing a group of potential lawyers around on 9 July 1993, when he decided to do his shtick. The first run and jump at a window went as planned, by which I mean he ran and twatted himself on the window like a confused elk, while a group of potential employees questioned the decisions that had led to this absolute window smear potentially becoming their boss. The

175

window held on the first try, but rather than leave it there old Garry decided to take another run at it.

Technically – and I'm really speaking technically here – he was correct, and had demonstrated that the window would not break, and I hope that gave him some solace as he knocked the window out of the frame entirely and plunged twenty-four storeys to his death. I've timed the fall and that's roughly enough time to sing 'It's like an unbreakable windooooooow that you smashed out the frame' to the tune of Alanis Morissette's 'Ironic' before it's time to meet your maker. After his death, a structural engineer told the *Toronto Star*, 'I don't know of any building code in the world that would allow a 160-pound man to run up against a glass and withstand it.'[101]

While this was bad for Garry, being dead, it also wasn't great for the law firm, who genuinely had to put out a statement to the *Toronto Sun* that he – the guy that had just run at a window like a raccoon trapped in a car – was 'one of the best and brightest' at the firm. The company didn't survive long afterwards.

PEPSI ONCE HAD THE SIXTH BIGGEST NAVY IN THE WORLD

People bang on about the East India Trading Company, but did you know that right under our modern noses, Pepsi briefly had the sixth biggest naval fleet in the world? In 1989, the beverage company owned a fleet of Soviet warships. Yet they didn't even seize the opportunity to rid the world of Coca-Cola, or take out a few of the poxier lemonades.

So how did a beverage company that's never assaulted anything other than your teeth, taste buds, pancreas and bowels, come to have a navy that could wipe out most countries in the world? Flash back to 1959. President Dwight D. Eisenhower wanted to ease relations between America and the Soviet Union. He created the American National Exhibition, in Moscow, to which America took all their best gadgets and products and displayed them in stalls in front of a Soviet crowd and their premier, Steve Buscemi from *The Death of Stalin*, while explaining a bit about them. Items included washing machines, Polaroid cameras and Vice President Richard Nixon. It was like the QVC channel, but with the possibility that it could end in nuclear Armageddon.

Coca-Cola had declined to participate in the exhibition, but one of the organisers decided against their better judgement that, yes, Pepsi was OK, and they tagged along. It was Pepsi's ideal market, where absolutely nobody had tasted any other cola and so didn't know Pepsi was irredeemably awful and not even rescuable by adding milk.[102] They had a plan: the head of Pepsi's international division requested that, when Nixon walked around with Steve Buscemi (better known as Khrushchev), he would take the Soviet leader to a booth where Pepsi was being served. There, he would be photographed drinking a cup, which would be seen back in the US. I wonder why they so consistently lose out to Coca-Cola when they have such brilliant strategies as telling 1950s Americans 'Try Pepsi, Commies love it!'

Khrushchev had his Pepsi, as did a lot of members of the public who attended the fair. Khrushchev's son, Sergei, described the reaction to the product, saying 'Everybody remembered Pepsi-Cola, it smelled like shoe wax,'[103] which wasn't a great start, but was correct. They developed a taste for it, though, and Pepsi would soon have a monopoly in the Russian cola market. In 1972, they struck a deal with the USSR to ship in their syrup, which would then be mixed locally with water, creating the first capitalist product to be sold in the Soviet Union.

The problem was that the Soviet currency was absolutely worthless internationally at the time, so a different type of payment had to be made. The Soviet Union began trading vodka for Pepsi, which in terms of swapsies is like trading a four-bedroom house in Mayfair for Alf Pogs. They carried on trading like this until they hit another snag in 1989, when America boycotted Soviet vodka following the Soviet–Afghan war, making trading for vodka completely useless.

Instead, they hit on one of the weirdest deals in history. Pepsi would take seventeen submarines, a frigate, a cruiser and a destroyer in return for ... syrup. They would then sell on the boats to make money, and so briefly became owners of the sixth biggest navy in the world, shortly before they secured their status as one of the world's biggest arms dealers/disarmers of a global superpower. The trade, worth $3 billion, went ahead, and for a brief moment Coca-Cola must have been shitting themselves at the implied threat. However, once the Soviet Union collapsed, Coca-Cola flooded the market and people immediately put down their shoe wax.

But the next time you ask for Coke and a member of the bar staff replies, 'Is Pepsi OK?' you might want to think about their massive fleet of gunships before you tell them, understandably, that you'd rather drink your own piss.

THE MAN WHO CHUGGED
RADIATION JUICE TILL
HIS BONES FELL OFF

Until his death, Eben Byers was a wealthy industrialist who liked nothing better than womanising, playing golf, and chugging pint after pint of deadly uranium.

Byers was taking the sleeper train one day in 1927, when he fell from his bunk bed and injured his arm, which meant he could no longer play his favourite game of golf nor, one presumes, womanise with quite the gusto he'd once enjoyed. No sane doctors would help him, but thankfully this was the 1920s, when any old malt loaf who could afford a stethoscope and hold it together through med school could become a doctor and start peddling nonsense. In the nineteenth century, for instance, you could be prescribed heroin for a tickly cough or have your testicles electrocuted to 'cure' your impotence, probably permanently. The 'doctor' that Eben went for was William Bailey, a man who hadn't even bothered to do the medical school bit and had decided instead to just say he had, before selling things like rat poison as an aphrodisiac. Bailey gave Byers a bottle of his patented 'Radithor', which was basically just radium squash.

This wasn't the only radioactive product on sale at the time. In

1896, radioactivity had been discovered, and before anyone could say 'Now let's cool our tits for a bit and check if this glowing rock gives anyone cancer,' people were smearing it all over their skin like they were about to lose it, which they were. In Germany you could get your hands on Doramad Radioactive Toothpaste if you wanted to give your teeth a clean and fresh 'I'm going to die soon, aren't I' feel. Your teeth would shine, sure, but because of radiation sickness they would no longer be attached to your mouth. There were also radioactive earplugs, blankets – and laxatives, in case you fancied trying to give your arsehole superpowers.

Eben, being very vanilla, stuck to his Chernobylade and swore by the stuff. After his arm started to feel better (probably by co-incidence) he kept drinking the juice in large quantities, necking about three bottles of it a day over the course of three years. Not one to hog all the poison, he also sent cases to his girlfriends and business partners and encouraged them to chug the stuff too. He even gave it to his horses. At the time, the full health risks of radi-ation weren't known. Regulators weren't convinced of the harm-ful effects, and even took action against one maker of radioactive 'medicines' because they hadn't put in as much deadly radioactive materials as they'd promised, like a poison victim complaining to their host that they'd been stiffed on the cyanide.

Several years into this routine (akin to popping off to Fukush-ima for a swim every couple of days), Eben began not to feel so good. He developed aches and pains all over his body, as well as massive headaches, all of which were difficult to concentrate on when his teeth began to fall out and his bones started to disin-tegrate. The radium he had been slurping like a delicious Yazoo had accumulated in his bones over the years, and now they were *crumbling*.[104]

182

Regulators had begun to cotton on to the fact that people exposed to radiation tended to die a bit, and they asked if he wouldn't mind coming along and testifying to that effect. But unfortunately by that point he was far too ill for the trip. A lawyer sent to write a report on him told the inquiry that Byers' 'whole upper jaw, excepting two front teeth, and most of his lower jaw had been removed'. In addition, the lawyer reported, 'all the remaining bone tissue of his body was disintegrating, and holes were actually forming in his skull.'

His death was as certain as it was grim. After the inevitable took place in 1932, and his body was placed in a lead coffin, his teeth and a bit of his remaining jawbone were placed on unexposed film. The film lit up like it was under an X-ray machine.[105]

Following his demise, many doctors (the real kind, not the ones who saw an arm bruise and prescribed cancer) testified about the ill effects of radiation, eventually leading, in the end, to the closure of the radioactive quackery industry. The inventor of Radithor, meanwhile, insisted that his drink was safe until his death from bladder cancer in 1949. When medical researchers dug up his corpse twenty years later, his insides were 'ravaged' by radiation, and, according to the team, *still warm*.

THE SUBMARINE CAPTAIN THAT SHAT HIS CREW TO DEATH

There are all kinds of things that can go wrong when you step inside a big metal tube and sink yourself to the bottom of the ocean, mocking God, Poseidon and dolphins as you do so.

Submarines have existed since Alexander the Great, before Jesus was even a twinkle in his daddy's eye. Back then they were incredibly basic. If you could sit in a big jar and make it sink for a while, people would look at you like you'd just morphed into shark form before their very eyes. According to accounts and a crude painting of old Alex himself being lowered into one of these tubs, he used them to scout out enemy land. Roll on a millennium and the Greeks were still at it, as this report published in 1562 states: 'Two Greeks submerged and surfaced in the river Tagus near the City of Toledo several times in the presence of The Holy Roman Emperor Charles V, without getting wet and with the flame they carried in their hands still alight.' Quite what intelligence you can pick up while bobbing up and down like a well-lit and suspiciously large jar of pickle is something we can only speculate on. Things moved on slowly for the submarine, and by the American Civil War they were using hand-cranked propellers that could move a ship at about 3.5 horsepower, assuming your crew could crank with their hands at around 3.5 horsepower.

By the time World War II came around, most of the kinks had been ironed out. The hand crank was replaced with engines. They'd figured out that you couldn't emerge from the water too quickly or you'd get the bends, something they'd learnt largely by repeatedly getting the bends and also by deliberately giving animals the bends. It was at this point in time that submarines first had the classic little periscope that pops its head out of the water.

What they hadn't quite figured out was the toilet situation.[106]

Allied submarines at the time still used septic tanks, and stored up the poo until they could get rid of it after their mission. Nazi subs meanwhile would flush the poo directly into the sea, which I know isn't the worst thing about them but it speaks volumes about their attitudes that they were willing to shit on fish.

Both systems posed problems. Allied troops were using up precious space and weight by collecting their own poo like Ash collects Pokémon.[107] The Nazis were unable to fire out their poo deep underwater, due to the pressure (of the sea, not the performance), meaning they'd have to save it all up in a bucket until they were high enough in the water to fire it out on fish just trying to enjoy their day. Though don't feel too sad for the fish. Their neutrality in the face of such times also speaks volumes about whether they're the kind of marine life that deserve to avoid being shat on.

The need to come up to the surface to empty waste could be a deadly one, as subs relied on being deep enough underwater to go undetected. And so the Nazis came up with a new system for their German Type VIIC vessel, which would allow them to release their business while still under high pressure: the poop was taken through a series of chambers, ending in an airlock. Picture an astronaut moving about a space station, but it's a poo. In this final airlock, the waste would get shot out with pressurised air into the sea. The system was incredibly complicated for a toilet, and required each sub to have a toilet specialist, which is a hell of a title to go on your CV. The toilet guy would open and close the valves in the right order, to make sure the poo – or worse, the water outside – didn't make its way onto the ship.

On the maiden voyage of the U-1206, however, Captain Karl-Adolf Schlitt decided that he, a captain, didn't require the help of a toilet specialist in order to do the task he'd been doing for most of his life. It went wrong, of course, and he was forced to ask an engineer to help him flush. The engineer also got things wrong, and before they knew it raw sewage was heading back through the toilet, shortly followed by the ocean. The captain's poo they were wading in was, understandably, the least of their concerns right now, as the liquid began to leak through the floor onto the batteries stored below. It reacted with the chemicals in the batteries, and soon the submarine began filling with chlorine gas.

The captain, probably while saying 'No time to explain' in order to avoid having to explain he'd shat on the batteries and now everyone was going to die, ordered the crew to begin ascending. It was a desperate scramble to the surface, so they blew the ballast tanks and even fired off all their torpedoes to make themselves lighter, as the ship continued to flood.

They reached the surface, but before the captain could even open the hatch and say 'I'd leave it a few minutes if I were you,' Allied planes spotted the sub and began to bomb the crap out of it, which would have solved the problem in the first place. The crew fled the submarine on dinghies but were captured the moment they made it to land. Meanwhile four of the crew died, having been killed by their captain's need for a number two and (I'm speculating wildly here) his embarrassment at having to get a crew member to flush down his massive log.

AVOID THE NOID

In the 1980s, an era devoid of artistic merit when *Mannequin* was considered a 'film' and Rick Astley was allowed to roam free, Domino's Pizza came up with one of the worst ad campaigns in history.

McDonald's had the Hamburglar, a man who would steal hamburgers, apparently unaware of their decline in value when you try to resell them from a sack. Adverts would feature the Hamburglar trying to nick hamburgers, only to be foiled and thrown in the slammer by Ronald McDonald, appealing to the demographic that wants hamburgers guarded under an aggressive security regime.

Inexplicably, Domino's Pizza saw this and thought they'd invent their own cartoon character that was constantly trying to disrupt the workings of their restaurant. A tiny red man in skin-tight Spandex with antennae that tries to stop delivery people from delivering pizzas was born. For unknown reasons, this strange alien freak was fucking livid at the very idea of anybody getting themselves hot pizza, and would do anything to make it stop. The ad agency came up with the slogan 'Avoid the Noid', probably just because 'Noid' rhymes with 'avoid' and the advertisers weren't willing to look for another rhyme. It was very much from the 'fuck it, that'll do' school of advertising that came up with 'Don't mind if I Baileys'.

The Noid was annoying, but so was everything in the eighties. Just look at Chris de Burgh or Jimmy Savile. What elevated the Noid to a strange cult status was an incident beyond the control of Domino's or any of their advertising team. On 30 January 1989, Kenneth Lamar Noid (well, fuck me, it is a real name) entered a branch of Domino's Pizza and took everyone inside hostage.[108] The man believed that the Noid adverts (and their slogan about avoiding the Noid) were aimed at him specifically, probably because nobody else on Earth has that name. He demanded $100,000 for the release of the hostages as well as a library book, but the employees were able to slip out, distracting him with two hot pizzas.

Ironically, he had disrupted service at Domino's Pizza in exactly the way the non-Kenneth Noid would have done. Domino's terrible advertising campaign was discontinued shortly afterwards, though they deny it had anything to do with being so awful the main thing anyone remembers about it was that it accidentally led to a hostage situation.

THIS IS HOW SOME ANIMALS
CRANK ONE OUT

L ook, the title of the book promised you there'd be stuff you don't want to know, and I'm nothing if not honest. Maybe you don't want to know it because it's grim, maybe because it's awkward, or maybe because it makes you picture Flipper jacking off using the body of a dead fish. If you received this book as a gift, Merry Christmas by the way.

Porcupines

In 1946, back when showing a bit of knee was on a par with telling colleagues to check out your PornHub comments, American biologist Albert R. Shadle described what happened between two porcupines in his care. In separate cages during mating season, the female porcupine displayed itself to the male. Unable to move any closer, the male began to masturbate furiously.

How do these famously quite spiky creatures masturbate, you ask? Carefully.

I joke, it merely fucked everything in sight. It banged its food and it banged its water, inadvertently proving that, as well as being wankers, porcupines don't really plan ahead for mealtimes. After having a go at the wire cage and deciding that it wasn't pleasurable – even though what is pleasurable for a porcupine is essentially porking a pincushion – it held a stick with its two front hands and used that to massage its penis to completion.[109]

Walruses

Walruses make the list because it's fun to picture. You know how seals can clap with their hands? Well, walruses can do that but a lot lower down, if you know what I mean. As well as being able to grab their penis using their flippers, the walruses can also perform oral sex on themselves, avoiding their giant tusks like a seasoned pro.

Spider monkeys

You know how in school one creepy kid would always mention that they sat on their hand before masturbation, to make it feel like somebody else was capable of treating them with anything but disgust? Well, spider monkeys can use their prehensile tails to give themselves a reach around.[110] True artists of the genre.

Horses

Cursed with hooves instead of fingers, horses are much less so-phisticated, and just sort of wave their penises around, slapping them on their stomach in the hope of achieving something. It doesn't often lead to completion, but it's the participation that counts.[111]

Dolphins

And now we move on to Flipper. I'm not sure why they left it out of the movie – maybe it's somewhere in the director's cut, or it was removed from the film so the certificate could be downgraded from an 18 to a U – but dolphins have been caught on camera mas-turbating by having sex with a decapitated fish head using their long, prehensile penis.

These fish actually escaped pretty lightly. Dolphins have been observed masturbating using the mouth of a live, panicked eel. This also didn't make the movie, even though it really could have added some drama to act three.

MORE ALLIES MAY HAVE BEEN KILLED TRAINING FOR D-DAY THAN ON ACTUAL D-DAY

Much like *Les Misérables* and *Shrek the Musical*, a lot of the real hard work of war goes on behind the scenes. You don't just rock up on opening night and expect to play Jean Valjean or the far more complex character of Donkey with no preparation whatsoever, so why would you expect to reclaim Normandy with the same attitude?

No, many months and years are put into preparing for such events, and D-Day was no exception. Allied troops were put through intense training ahead of the landings, which was much more realistic than most. Everything had to be lifelike, from the beach they were landing on, to the conditions they'd face when they arrived, to the massive death toll of Allied troops they'd endure.

During Operation Overlord, the preparations for D-Day, historian Peter Caddick-Adams estimates that more Allied lives were lost than during actual D-Day,[112] across a series of unfortunate and avoidable incidents that make *A Series Of Unfortunate Events* look like the day 'Perfect Day' was flapping on about.

Probably the biggest screw-up was Exercise Tiger, which turned out to be a lot more dangerous than letting an actual tiger exercise in a nursery. On 27 April 1942, a practice assault was scheduled at Slapton Sands, Devon. In order to grow accustomed to the conditions of battle, General Dwight D. Eisenhower (yes, that one) ordered that the dress rehearsal contain live ammunition, like a theatre director insisting that the first read-through be attended by the critics and everyone's dads.

The plan was that warships would open fire on the beach an hour before the fake landing took place, to familiarise everyone with the smells of shelling without actually shelling them.[113] The problem was several of the ships that were supposed to land that day were delayed. It was decided that they would put back the whole thing by an hour to give them time to catch up. Inevitably some of the landing ships hadn't received word of the change, and so showed up on the beach as scheduled, which happened to be right at the time when the rearranged bombing of the beach was to occur. The men, who had been expecting a fake landing on a beach in order to practise avoiding their deaths at the hands of the enemy, now found themselves on a beach having the crap shelled out of them by themselves. Eyewitnesses to the events told the *Observer* many years later that, as well as shelling from behind, the men landing in the fake D-Day landings faced allies posing as Germans firing at them, and for some unfathomable reason (other than maybe they went full method) they had been given live ammo. 'We later found out it was a mistake,' one Royal Engineer told the newspaper.[114] 'They should have had dummy ammunition, but they just carried on shooting.'

It's thought that around 450 men were killed that day. We had Daniel Day Lewis-ed the fuck out of ourselves in our bizarre need to prioritise realism over keeping enough troops alive for the enemy to shoot at.

THE POPES WHO ARE DEFINITELY GOING TO HELL

Nowadays, the Pope is seen by much of the world as a sort of benign grandpa figure. You might not want to get into a debate with one on the necessities of abortion, and you might be a bit scared to introduce another to your same-sex partner in case he gave 'the hellfire speech' – but most of the time popes are regarded as Santas with shit hats.

In the early days of the papacy, however, it was basically like a spaghetti western but presumably with actual spaghetti. As well as the numerous poisonings of popes, sometimes followed by hammerings (Pope John VIII was poisoned by one of his own clerics, but they grew tired of waiting for him to die and twatted him to death with a hammer), the popes were also horny as the hell they believed they'd end up in.

The sex pope

It's a shame that popes aren't named like medieval kings (such as Ethelred the Unready, who was shit at leaving the house on time), instead sticking to a handful of names from a grammar school playground followed by Roman numerals to look fancy. Otherwise we could have been treated to names such as Benedict the Horny,

Benedict the Hornier Still and Benedict Look I Know We Said That Last One Was Horny But This One Will Pork Anything.

The horniest of all the popes was probably Pope Benedict IX. Though many of the popes had male and female lovers, Pope Benedict IX, according to accounts by Pope Victor III,[115] sponsored and hosted a lot of orgies, routinely had sex, and committed 'rapes, murders and other unspeakable acts. His life as a pope so vile, so foul, so execrable, that I shudder to think of it,'[116] though others did think of it without shuddering and noted that he liked a bit of bestiality too. St Peter Damian, an actual saint, said he was 'a demon from hell in the disguise of a priest' while mentioning the bestiality thing, which is fair enough. Eventually in 1048, Benedict decided he'd had enough of poping and wanted to marry his cousin, so he sold the papacy to his godfather in exchange for a big pile of gold.

The gravedigging pope

In January 897, Pope Stephen VI dug up the corpse of a previous pope and put the skeleton on trial.

Power struggles between popes had been raging for some time before they escalated into a good old-fashioned corpse trial, but not enough to really justify the spectacle. The pope on trial – Pope Formosus – had possibly been killed by poison, and he was succeeded by Boniface VI who was subsequently also possibly killed by poison fifteen days after becoming pope, when he was still settling in and getting used to the 'big hat'. Things were pretty tense, and if you were the Pope you'd sure as hell keep an eye on your glass or you'd soon earn yourself an early ticket to Saintsville.

In a particularly unhinged act, during what is now known as the Cadaver Synod, Pope Stephen, who succeeded Boniface, took the body of Pope Formosus and placed it in a chair in a church at San Giovanni in Laterano. All the priests were there watching as the Pope yelled accusations of blasphemy at the body of a former pope who had been undressed and redressed in his formal papal vestments. The dead pope was allowed a lawyer, but failed to mount a defence to Pope Stephen's unhinged yelling. Once you've stripped a dead pope bollock naked and dressed him up for a trial, I guess there's no real point in holding back for decorum's sake. Dead pope was found guilty and had his papacy removed from him, before he was stripped butt naked once more and dressed in poor people clothes and thrown in a pauper's grave. Pope Stephen also had three fingers chopped off the corpse, despite it being a pretty ineffective way to punish someone that no longer has brain impulses to control those fingers, what with being a spooky ghost.

Not quite done yet, Stephen dug up the body once more and had it thrown in the River Tiber. However, old corpse pope got the last laugh, as his supporters imprisoned Stephen VI and strangled him to death a few months later, making the score roughly one-all, give or take a few corpse strippings.

THE SURGEON WHO'D
AMPUTATE YOUR LEGS AND
TAKE A LITTLE TESTICLE OFF
WHILE HE WAS THERE

If someone was to ask you what your priorities were during surgery, you'd probably say something like 'I'd like not to die, please.' The one thing you wouldn't say is 'Doctor, I want you to prioritise speed over everything else. I don't care if you accidentally chop off my face if it means you also slice thirty seconds off your personal best.' Enter surgeon Robert Liston in 1835, carrying a stopwatch and looking like he's got someplace else to be.

Doing speedy surgery was a priority back in the days when there were no anaesthetics. You don't have to have a medical degree to know that the less time a patient spends staring at their own leg getting sawn off, the less chance they have of going into shock. You also didn't necessarily have to have a medical degree to saw legs off back then either, so that was lucky.

Robert Liston, Professor of Clinical Surgery at University College Hospital in London, had a reputation for being incredibly speedy at amputations, and for having a remarkably good survival rate for his patients. If you went to see him, there was a five in six chance you'd make it out of there alive.[117] Which today would get you investigated by the medical authorities, but back then basically made you Jesus.

He was a bit arrogant with it. You don't kill just ten out of sixty-six patients with a saw in five years without getting a bit big-headed. He would stride into the surgery room, put on a clean apron and even *wash his hands* with a flourish. Though expected today, back then hand washing was a bit decadent, the equivalent of demanding a bubble bath before you perform an appendectomy. His students would hold down the patient and make sure any other limbs they wished to keep were as far away from the 'to saw' area as possible. Often asking his students to 'time me, gentlemen', Liston would then set about sawing through flesh, bone, and flesh again, before closing the wound in thirty seconds to three minutes, depending on different accounts. He earned the nickname 'the fastest knife in the west end', and surgeons would pack into his operating theatres to watch him go to town on a leg.

Unfortunately for the patients, speed occasionally comes at a bit of a price. During one surgery, it's said that Liston, while trying to keep his time down as usual, cut off the testicles of the man he was operating on while trying to remove his leg. Seeing the time on the stopwatch was probably of little consolation to the patient. He also misidentified a boy's aneurysm of the carotid artery as a skin abscess, and stabbed the aneurysm with a knife he happened to have in his waistcoat pocket, killing the boy soon afterwards.

In another incident, for which he's better known, he's said to have conducted the only surgery with a 300 per cent mortality rate. The tale goes (though I suspect this is just a horror story spread around at the time to draw attention to his haphazard 'if I cut something off they should think of it as a bonus' attitude to major amputations, rather than actually being true) that he was meant to be amputating the leg of a patient. The person holding down the patient got a little too close to Liston's saw and, in his frenzy to cut off the leg, Liston chopped the other guy's fingers off, and they dropped in the debris pile with the leg. In the carnage,[118] as Liston brought his surgical knife back up, he's said to have accidentally slashed the coat of a spectator, who died of fright and became victim number one. Shortly afterwards, both the patient and Liston's assistant died of gangrene, which is much more believable than somebody willing to attend an amputation suddenly getting spooked to death by a knife.

The worst bit about the story of Robert Liston is that he was one of the better doctors, and people were willing to go to him like a maverick cop on seventies TV. He may not play by the rules, he may be a bit of a rogue, he may chop your testicles off while aiming for your index fingers, but my god he gets the job done.

After Liston's death, a marble statue of him was erected by his fellow surgeons, perhaps the only statue in existence of a man who once sliced off someone's testicles in a rush.

CAT BURNING: A PRELUDE TO SCRABBLE

Cats started off so well. Not in the film version – that was bafflingly awful from start to finish – but in the history of the world. Worshipped in Ancient Egypt and pulling chariots for Norse goddesses, they had a long way to fall, I guess. Now all they have left is the odd gif and the horrors of former national treasure Ian McKellen doing an impression of them lapping milk out of a bowl.

But it turns out they have damn good reason to be so aloof towards humans. While we were becoming best friends with dogs, humans apparently wanted to make it clear this was an exclusive relationship by being extra special shits to cats, as you're about to find out.

Brûler les chats

You don't have to know much French to guess that brûler is something you don't want to do to chats. Either you know it means 'burning', or you're picturing a cat baked into a crème brûlée, which might be worse. In medieval France, though, it was the height of entertainment to set fire to cats, whether in a sack suspended over a fire, in cages, or just by soaking the poor thing in flammable liquid, setting fire to it and chasing it through the streets. One of the reasons suggested for why they did this is that cats were the sign of the devil, but my guess is that this is just the sort of pastime you resort to when your culture has thus far failed to invent *Come Dine With Me*.

Old head cat smash

Another favourite hobby of medieval Europe – this time in Italy – was for villagers to grab a cat and nail it to a tree, still alive. While you might have a bit of a cry about what's just happened or seek immediate therapy, the medievallers were only just beginning. This part, to them, was like getting the Monopoly board out of the box. They would then try and kill the cat by thwacking it to death with their heads, while the cat – understandably – attempted to claw their faces off.[119] People would play trumpets while this was all going on, which must have just rubbed it in to the dying cats' faces that the villagers *did* have other forms of entertainment, they just preferred to headbutt them to death like a mad bull.

The cat trials

Back in France, in 1730, they'd moved on from burning cats for fun and were now hanging them out of vengeance. Ah, the march of human progress.

In Paris, two apprentice printers wanted to get their own back on their masters. Rather than the advanced and sophisticated methods we have today (like shitting in the boss's desk), the duo decided to convince their masters that their beloved cats were possessed by the devil.[120] Remarkably, rather than being told to lay off the syphilis, the owners believed them, and allowed them to stage a trial of the cats, who stupidly decided to represent themselves in court. The cats were condemned to death and hanged, all to annoy their owners.

Monkey bomb

Technically not a cat (bit of trivia for you there), but during the Opium Wars the Chinese planned to strap monkeys to fireworks and throw them into British ships to cause chaos. It's not clear whether they were motivated by a need to cause maximum carnage or merely by an excess of monkeys, but the idea was the monkeys would freak out and end up setting fire to important parts of the ship. No doubt this would have worked spectacular-ly, but the plan hit a snag when nobody was willing to get close enough to lob a monkey into a ship.[121]

THE KENTUCKY MEAT SHOWER

On 9 March 1876, it rained beef in Kentucky.

A woman named Mrs Crouch, forgotten from the annals of history (bar that one time when beef pissed down on her house), was outside in her yard making soap. Which was handy, because shortly afterwards she heard the unmistakable slapping sound of beef landing on the floor around her. The sky, the *New York Times* reported,[122] was perfectly clear at the time, which is even more mysterious than if she had looked up and seen a beef cloud, or had earlier heard her husband say, 'Looks like it's going to beef it down later,' while clocking a particularly beefy-looking rump of cloud in the distance.

Mrs Crouch, who we may as well call Mrs Beef from now on given that no other record of her exists, told reporters that it covered an area of more than 100 feet and fell like large snowflakes, though some of the chunks were about three or four inches square. Decent chunks you might use in a stir fry if they hadn't fallen to the ground like they'd been shat out by God. Two 'gentlemen' decided to try the mystery meat, which, according to the *New York Times*, they described as 'perfectly fresh', as if that was the main query the men had. 'You know what, I would absolutely love to scoff down this sky meat, Margaret, but I do believe it's a tad past its sell-by date.' When they tasted it, they described it as either mutton or venison.

So, what the hell was going on? First off, the *New York Times* described Mrs Beef as 'unquestionable'. This was the kind of woman to whom, if she says 'it's raining beef out there', you nod, and say 'Well, I'd better fetch me a beef umbrella then hadn't I, Mrs Beef,' rather than, for instance, 'No it isn't, shut up.' So something happened here that made it rain miscellaneous types of meat, there's no question of that.

Samples were eventually analysed in a more scientific manner than two random gentlemen putting it in their mouths. It was sent to Dr A. Mead Edwards, who said that it was either the lung tissue of a horse or a human infant, which was corroborated by others.[123] Mystery solved, if your curiosity only stretches to establishing whether it was or wasn't sirloin.

Later that year, Dr L. D. Kastenbine proposed what is likely the actual explanation after examining the meat (which he deduced to be mutton) himself. 'The only plausible theory explanatory of this anomalous shower appears to me to be that suggested by the old Ohio farmer,' he wrote in *Louisiana Medical News*.[124] 'The disgorgement of some vultures that were sailing over the spot, and from their immense height the particles were scattered by the then prevailing wind over the ground.'

When vultures eat, they gorge themselves, not knowing when they are going to eat again. Though necking food like this is a fine way to live (trust me), it isn't exactly great for flight. If they are startled, say, after a group of them have eaten a big old sheep, they will barf everywhere when they fly. Rather than some strange mystery, all that had happened was a bunch of vultures puked up a rancid sheep and a couple of blokes later gave it a bit of a chew.

ANTI-TANK DOGS

During World War II, as the Nazis advanced on Moscow in 1941, Soviet troops became desperate. They lacked anti-tank weapons to deal with (as the name implies) tanks that the Nazis were using. The tanks were vulnerable from below, but other than lying in a ditch waiting for a tank to go over you like a paparazzi creep waiting for Beyoncé, there weren't many ways you could get under there and, importantly, make it out alive. Enter man's best friend, looking pleased to see us and unaware we are about to blow it to smithereens.[125]

The Russians came up with an idea that, while in theory would work, would also lose them quite a bit of the moral high ground and condemn them all to hell. They would train dogs to run underneath tanks with bombs strapped to their backs, where they would explode both themselves and the tanks.

To train the dogs, they had to be cruel to the poor things, of course. Don't look at me like that – did you honestly think a story about Russians blowing dogs into tiny dog meat chunks was going to be cruelty-free? The first stage involved convincing dogs that they wanted to climb underneath a death machine, when most animals – another bit of trivia for you – will avoid imminent death wherever possible. This they did by starving the dogs, before placing dog food beneath some tanks during training. The hungry puppers would then learn that food could be found beneath tanks, and would run under there, blissfully unaware they were rehearsing their own demise. An antenna on their back would trigger the bomb as it brushed the underside of the tank.

The next step was to recreate a proper war environment for the dogs to become accustomed to, so they wouldn't be fazed by extracting their lunch under fire, which sounds bad when you're human but must be confusing as hell when you're a dog unaware of the concept of forks, let alone of war.

I don't know why – maybe I'm just hungry – but the food aspect seems especially cruel in all of this. The poor dogs thought they were about to be fed, not have their limbs scattered 100m into the air. If you need an analogy to get your empathy juices flowing, it would be like a waiter telling you, 'I'm going to bring you some lovely soup now,' and then stabbing you in the chin.

Despite their training, in the real battle situation the dogs were too frightened by the loud noises and their dog friends being killed to really worry about kibble. There are urban legends that the Russian tanks the dogs were trained on were diesel, whereas the German tanks ran on petrol, so the dogs darted back towards the diesel smell and blew the crap out of the Russian tanks. This last part is untrue, but the diesel did confuse the shit out of the dogs to much the same effect. With the confusion, the noise and the Germans attempting to kill the dogs, it all ended up in inevitable disaster. 'Most of the dogs refuse to work and aim to jump back inside the trench,' one handler wrote in October 1941.[126] 'Nine dogs ran to the targets, but then got scared by explosions around them and tried to hide. Three of them exploded, two were never found, the rest had to be destroyed by us because they were running back to us.'

The Germans became wise to the tactic, and began executing strays on sight, all in all making it a very confusing time for dogs. The system was soon changed, both because the Russians finally created more effective anti-tank weapons than a frightened dog fitted with TNT and a tendency to return to its owner, and because it was sapping Russian morale that they now either had to blow the shit out of dogs, or execute them for absconding.

THE FIRST EVER MOONING REPORTEDLY LEFT THOUSANDS DEAD

Some inventions are so obvious in retrospect that if the inventor was to run in excitedly and show it to you, your first reaction wouldn't be 'Well done you,' but more 'Why the fuck didn't you think of this before, Einstein?'

The can opener, for instance, was invented nearly fifty years after the can.[127] The tin was made in 1795, but until 1858 you would sit there hungry and have to smash it open with a hammer and chisel to get to your ye olde beans. I can't imagine feeling anything other than pure rage and the need to scream 'WHERE THE HELL WERE YOU BEFORE, MAN, I'M COVERED IN SOUP!' at the person who showed up fifty years later to announce I'd been doing it like an idiot all this time.

Speaking of cans, the weirdest of all the late inventions for me has to be the concept of mooning. It took until AD 80 for humans to develop the art of getting your bum out and waggling it at an enemy in order to insult them. The butt cheeks and, indeed, their friend the anus, have been following us around for hundreds of thousands of years, and yet it wasn't until one fateful day in that year (the first record of a mooning, I should point out;

it's possible there were earlier moons that are lost to time like tears in rain) that one Roman soldier decided, 'I'm going for it,' and pulled back his garment, which was the olden-times way of dropping trow.

The soldier, according to a first-century historical account in *The Jewish War*, waved his bum at a group of Jewish people celebrating Passover at a temple. 'One of the soldiers pulled back his garment and, cowering down after an indecent manner, turned his breech to the Jews, and spake such words as you might expect upon such a posture,' Flavius Josephus wrote in his account of the mooning.[128] It's widely believed that 'spaking' in this context means farting, an aspect of the art of mooning that has been sadly lost through the generations.

The crowds did not take kindly to the gesture. Despite it being the early days of the moon, they correctly identified it as an unfriendly greeting, or maybe even as an unorthodox way of saying 'happy Passover' despite containing three of the necessary letters. 'At this' – 'this' being the bum waggling – 'the whole multitude had indignation, and made a clamour to Cumanus – the Roman procurator of Iudaea Province – that he would punish the soldier; while the rasher part of the youth, and such as were naturally the most tumultuous, fell to fighting, and caught up stones, and threw them at the soldiers.'

Fearing for his own safety, Cumanus – who, surprise surprise, was on the mooner's side, having as he did the name Cum anus – sent for armed soldiers to fight the crowds, rather than just ask the one soldier to apologise for the fart. The gathered crowds were beaten out of the temple and ran for the city. In the violence and stampede caused by a visible ass, they trod on and were crushed into each other so badly that – according to

Josephus – ten *thousand* people were killed. In terms of pure effectiveness as a weapon, this man's ass would go unmatched until the invention of napalm.

DON'T BE AN ARSEHOLE TO STAFF; ARCHAEOLOGISTS WILL JUDGE YOU

Nowadays, if you want to complain it's as easy as tagging Coca-Cola into a tweet and calling them bellends. You move on with your day, safe in the knowledge that you made some poor social media manager out there a bit sad. Before this you'd have to fax complaints and call them 'ye olde bellends', as was the custom of the 1980s. Way back in 1750 BC, however, you'd have to *really* be pissed off in order to complain, because it involved taking a chisel and twatting your message into a stone.

The oldest complaint (that we know of) was found in the ancient city of Ur in what is now Iraq. (Side point, but imagine finding an ancient relic buried deep in the earth, feeling like Indiana Jones, then translating it to find it begins with 'Further to my previous relic . . .'). It was chiselled by a man named Nanni who we don't know much about, other than he was really fucking pissed off about a delivery.

Sometime that year, someone called Ea-nasir – who was basically the ancient Iraqi equivalent of Yodel, if his customer service is anything to go by – had allegedly royally fucked up Nanni's order. I don't know why I said 'allegedly' there – if his mummified corpse wants to sue me, then come at me, bro.

Ea-nasir had also been a bit of a shit to Nanni's staff, which he was having none of. 'What do you take me for, that you treat somebody like me with such contempt?' he opened,[129] in what would nowadays read 'Oi, shithead'. 'I have sent as messengers gentlemen like ourselves to collect the bag with my money (deposited with you) but you have treated me with contempt by sending them back to me empty-handed several times, and that through enemy territory.

'Is there anyone among the merchants who trade with Telmun who has treated me in this way? You alone treat my messenger with contempt!' he continued, still twatting this out in the clay using a method which would have taken hours. The letter went on to demand repayment and insisted that he would not accept any more copper that wasn't up to his standards, and would inspect all his work individually and reject any he didn't like.

His letter finished. No other record of his life remains. This would be like if, thousands of years in the future, an advanced civilisation dug up CCTV footage of you telling the manager of Greggs their steak bake tastes like lukewarm human shit.

THE LAWYER WHO SHOT HIMSELF TO WIN A CASE

In 1870, in the town of Hamilton, Warren County, Ohio, a group of men were playing cards in the private room of a bar when a group of ruffians walked in. It was fightin' time. That's how it worked back then, apparently: you just walked into a room and if it was occupied it was time to punch a face in.

During this run-of-the-mill round of fisticuffs, one Thomas Myers attempted to draw out his trusty gun from his pocket and get real shooty (not everything was different, this was still America) when the group heard a muffled shot. Myers, maybe reacting to the shot, drew out his gun and quickly fired off a few rounds before falling down dead. Everybody fled the room, which must have been irritating for whoever was winning Uno, and in the chaos nobody really knew what happened.

However, they knew who to blame: Myers' nemesis, Thomas McGehan. Everyone had a nemesis back then; it was a much slower time where you could whittle away the hours really getting to hate a specific individual.

McGehan was put on trial, where he was represented by a lawyer that would do anything to win a case. Former Congressman Clement Vallandigham believed McGehan to be innocent, and held that Myers had accidentally shot himself while going for his pistol. He went out to conduct ballistics tests to see what residue was left on cloth when firing a pistol at close range.[130] He had three bullets left in the gun after the tests, when one of his colleagues told him, 'You had better discharge them.' At which point Clemmy (there's no way I'm typing out Vallandigham twice) told the man, 'I have carried and practised with pistols too long to be afraid to have a loaded one in my pocket.'[131] To be fair to the idiot, nobody had yet heard of Chekhov.

Back at his hotel room, he put the loaded gun down next to an unloaded gun that had been shown in court that day. Shortly afterwards, he picked up the wrong gun and decided to demonstrate to his fellow lawyers how he thought Myers had killed himself. He put the gun in his pocket before retrieving it.

'There,' he said in his moment of triumph, 'that's the way Myers held it.' Right before he shot himself like Myers did, and exclaimed 'My God, I've shot myself!' Which, again to be fair to the pie, did help prove the point. He died shortly afterwards, either pointlessly or having successfully hammered his argument home to get his client off, depending on your perspective. Before you feel too bad for him or declare him some sort of committed hero lawyer, I should mention he was a massive racist who, as a congressman, fought to continue slavery.

McGehan was released shortly after the incident, but remarkably, this wasn't the end of the shootings. At least, not according to the *Fife Herald*, which stated: 'Hardly was he in his grave before another man killed himself while trying precisely in the same way to demonstrate how Mr Vallandigham had met his death.'

It's unclear whether the killings stopped because someone stepped in and started supervising the idiots or because they simply ran out of bullets.

THE WAR ON SQUIRRELS
(FOUGHT BY KIDS)

In April 1918, while the world was at war, the children of California set about systematically slaughtering over 100,000 squirrels.

Californian ground squirrels were irritating little creatures that were causing havoc on farms in the state. Farmers were struggling to keep the pest at bay, and so the state organised 'squirrel week', which is a lot more genocidal than the adorable name implies. The plan was to conduct a week-long killing frenzy, in which people would go out and poison, bludgeon, shoot and drown the fuck out of these adorable little furries. And by people, I mean kids. The horticulture commissioner George H. Hecke wanted children to go into battle against the squirrels, at least giving them a fair chance, or figuring that it's best to get humans to go on killing frenzies before they've developed a functioning moral compass.

The problem was that if you tell kids 'Ah, it's mole-twatting week' or 'glass-a-bee Tuesday', they'll generally look at you like you've told them to take a chainsaw to Paddington Bear. Pre-empting this, the Californian government decided to launch an actual propaganda campaign against squirrels, in the same vein that they would eventually use against the Nazis.

In one leaflet you see what initially appears to be a nice picnic, until you look a little closer and see a woman is holding a bucket of poison and telling some kids 'We must kill the squirrels to save food, but use the poison carefully,' while, behind her, a child shoots a rifle and a toddler flails around with a baton. That was one of the subtle ones; another put German spiked army helmets on the squirrels, as well as Iron Crosses and Kaiser Wilhelm moustaches. If you're having trouble grasping how weird this is, imagine it today but it's badgers and they're dressed up like Osama Bin Laden.

Once the kids were on board (how could they not be with slogans like 'the BEST squirrel is the dead squirrel' and 'death to the squirrel'), they were set to work with their poisons. The commissioner made it into a competition, in which kids could win money for killing the most squirrels, solving the problem in the short term but inadvertently creating a 'we gave psychopaths a thirst for blood and taught them how to kill' problem a few years down the line.

The children were asked by the Californian government to bring the tails to school as proof of the kill and subsequent dis-memberment,[132] clearly learning fuck all from my Vietnamese rat-killing story – I don't know why I bother. The week-long fren-zy brought in an astonishing 104,509 tails.[133] The commissioner congratulated the children in the local paper for doing their 'patri-otic duty' and encouraged them to carry on doing it in their spare time for fun, now that the competition was over.

In some counties the killing continued unabated, with one frankly terrifying kid bringing in 3780 dead squirrels.[134] His parents apparently never sat him down and said 'Do ... do you not think three thousand cold-blooded kills is enough for now, Timmy? Maybe you could try playing tennis?'

THE ONLY WAY TO PROTECT OUR DESCENDANTS FROM OURSELVES IS TO SCARE THE SHIT OUT OF THEM

In Kesennuma, Japan, there are giant slabs of stone, some of which have been there for over 600 years. Quite terrifying to come across on a ramble, some of them explain that if you hear an earthquake you should flee for higher ground immediately. Each of them has been placed after a tsunami, in order to warn people years later not to build houses on the wrong side of the markers – nor use it as a place to chill after an earthquake.[135] The stones are a successful and deliberate attempt by people in the past to tell their descendants to stay the fuck away, and are a great example of what we should be doing as a species that's pumping out nuclear waste like there's no tomorrow.

Nuclear waste remains radioactive from 1,000 to 10,000 years. You can't just keep it out in the open (because of all the dying of radiation poisoning that tends to involve), so it gets buried away somewhere so awful that nobody will want to live there for 10,000 years, like Kent.

When Kent did this in 1981 (OK, it was Las Vegas, I just wanted to take another shit on Kent), a group of scientists, linguists, anthropologists and others gathered together to address a problem we'll have to take on at some point soon: How do we communicate mortal danger to a civilisation 10,000 years in the future?

As you'll find out by looking at literally any exhibit in the British Museum, simply placing your forbidden items in a large structure (such as the pyramids) will not keep the British from breaking the fucking door down and looting everything inside. As a general rule, if a human comes across a thing, their first instinct is to crack it open and worry about cursed mummies later, if *The Mummy* is anything to go by. To stick with the pyramid example for a moment (largely because I recently watched *The Mummy*), say you were the first person to come across it. You know no Ancient Egyptian. You could find yourself staring at hieroglyphics that read 'Be gone from here or suffer at the reanimated hands of Amenhotep' and as far as you're concerned all it says is 'Bird hand, bird, bird, man doing the walk like an Egyptian dance, bird, bird skull and crossbones'. Basically, if the Ancient Egyptians were trying to keep future people from digging up their graves, they did a terrible job – and should they ever spring back to life, their first act should be to feel thoroughly ashamed of themselves.

Hoping to do better than the Egyptians, the Human Interference Task Force decided they needed to convey three pieces of information to future generations who might stumble across the nuclear waste storage sites: 1, that what they are seeing is a message in the first place; 2, that there are dangerous materials stored near the message; 3, some basic information about what dangerous goo is stored there.

Here's where it gets batshit. Because there are so many variables (Will they speak the same language as us? Will our language survive 9,000 years? Will they even have language? Will dogs have taken over, meaning everything is now spelled 'woof'?), you are extremely limited in what you can convey, and how. You essentially either need to find something so universally understood that it could never lose its meaning across thousands of years, or a way of transferring knowledge that will endure. A bunch of solutions were suggested, with varying degrees of 'Stop huffing the paint, John, we're supposed to be doing a science' about them.

The Atomic Priesthood is obviously the standout of the bunch. Far from being radioactive priests, the atomic priesthood would be a group of appointed scientists responsible for ensuring that people did not go near the world's nuclear waste sites, both because they would probably die and because they might feasibly use them to make other people become dead too. In order to complete their task, they would have to make and consistently reinforce 'artificially created and nurtured ritual-and-legend, which would be a "false trail" for the uninitiated, who would be steered away from the hazardous site for reasons other than the scientific knowledge'.[136] Basically supernatural tales of why if you go near the site you are going to snuff it, without mentioning nuclear waste. Since even horror priests tend to die, the priests would replace themselves as they grew older, probably attributing their deaths to Cthulhu who lives in that strangely glowing nuclear storage facility down the road.

The strangest of the solutions (and that's saying something, given that the previous paragraph involved a cult of priests dedicated to spreading urban legends to scare the shit out of people thousands of years from now) was proposed by author Françoise Bastide and semiotician Paolo Fabbri. They believed the most sensible course of action was to breed 'radiation cats'[137] – i.e. cats

223

that would change colour and begin to glow when they came near radioactive material.

Making them glow is actually the easy part, and can be achieved by messing around with their genes a bit. The difficulty comes in trying to instil in everybody an innate fear of cats that change colour and glow. They too would create legends and folk-lore around glowing cats, informing people that the best course of action when a cat changes colour in front of you is to shit your-self and run away. Which, to be fair, is the only course of action available to you were that to happen. The idea was that the legend would be passed down through the generations in songs, poetry and music. Though the scientists failed to include descriptive lyr-ics that warned you to run when you saw a glowing cat, in a track that also happened to be an absolute banger.

One architect suggested creating fucked-up landscapes around the sites which would be 'non-natural, ominous, and re-pulsive',[138] suggesting things like bodily injury and wounding forms. It doesn't bode well for future civilisations that so many ideas to emerge from the brains trust essentially involved, in vari-ous ways, scaring the shit out of anybody who came near the site. The problem isn't going away, and so far the only one we aren't too embarrassed to actually try is merely updating the sign every now and then, and hoping that this will happen for millennia.

THE MAN WITH A HOLE IN HIS STOMACH, AND THE DOCTOR WHO DUG AROUND IN THERE

On 6 June 1822, just outside a trading post in Michigan, an accident occurred that would revolutionise medicine. This isn't one of those modern-day 'accidents' you read about where a physicist studying the mass of quarks accidentally measures the mass of a lepton – this was a proper, good old-fashioned accident where a man was blasted through the chest with a musket.

The injury to Alexis St Martin, a 19-year-old fur trapper from Canada, was grim. Really grim. Let's not beat about the bush, he had a hole in his chest out of which was hanging a bit of lung.[139] If you have an outside lung, generally you're about to have an outside soul to match.

As luck would have it, an army doctor – William Beaumont – was nearby and came when summoned. Now, I know that when you've got lung hanging out of you, you tend not to be too picky, but Alexis really should have asked a few questions, such as: (1) 'Are you the kind of guy who's going to leave a gaping hole in my chest and study me for a decade?' or (2) 'Are you sure there are no other doctors available?' Because the answer to question one is a massive yes.

Beaumont, to his credit, performed several surgeries on St Martin over the coming months in order to patch up his wound, after bleeding him of course. Back then, when somebody was losing blood, the solution was always to make them bleed more blood. But over the surgeries, he was able to save Alexis's life.

However, there was still a big hole in Alexis's chest. The edge of his stomach hole had joined up with his exterior hole, leaving a peephole into his stomach, ready for anybody to have a glance in there. The wound was kept sterile by his stomach acid, and, apart from the gigantic hole in his chest, he was pretty healthy.

That's a big caveat of course. You ask someone how they're doing and they say 'Fine, thanks, apart from this big fucking chasm in my chest,' you're pretty much obliged to ask, 'Are ... are you sure you're OK, mate?'

His digestive system was somehow still working, and Beaumont wanted to find out what was going on in there. Not much was known about either the stomach or digestion at the time, but it was assumed that the stomach merely pummelled the food (in a similar way to teeth) as a method of breaking it down. He offered Alexis a contract to stick around and have his hole studied, rather than go back to Canada. Alexis said yes because he was unable to carry on working as a trapper: it's hard to hunt when you're leaking juice out of your chest hole.

Yet St Martin really should have run a mile, and did on several occasions actually try to run away from Beaumont, though he returned when he ran out of money. Beaumont would give Alexis menial tasks in return for the money he needed, but he'd also give him food. Then, he'd start digging around in the hole to see what it looked like, which I'd say is a little on the familiar side from your boss.

'Dined at 3 o'clock – 30 minutes on beef soup, meat, and bread,' Beaumont wrote in his food diaries,[140] which sounds nice until you read the next sentence: '4 o'clock 14 minutes – took out a portion; particles of beef slightly macerated and partly digested. 5 o'clock 15 minutes – took out another portion.'

Beaumont studied Alexis for the best part of a decade, regularly taking food out of his hole and even putting into the hole food attached to a bit of string. While it's hard not to like somebody who's attaching beef to some twine and dipping it into your chest cavity like a tea bag, the two did not get on. Occasionally,

Beaumont would taste what he found in there, putting even more strain on the relationship.

The two carried on in this way, having tense meals followed by even tenser chest dives, and all the time irritating each other. Occasionally Beaumont would try and take Alexis on tours, giving lectures about him, during which St Martin actually tried to run away several times.[141] In terms of medical ethics, if your subject is trying to physically escape from you like you're a dog catcher in *101 Dalmatians*, you probably don't have what you could feasibly call 'informed consent'.

After ten years, Beaumont had enough research to prove that digestion was a chemical process, and St Martin was a free man. It was a hell of a breakthrough for the period, and many other scientists wanted to study St Martin, but he refused to let anybody else have a go on his hole, and returned to Canada where he lived for a surprisingly long time, dying aged seventy-eight after falling down some stairs. His family let his corpse rot at home for a bit,[142] making his body useless for any creeps who wanted to autopsy him, before burying him eight feet deep underground.

YOU'VE PROBABLY MADE OUT WITH A 160-YEAR-OLD DROWNING VICTIM

You may not have heard of *L'Inconnue de la Seine* (the unknown woman of the Seine), but there's a good chance you've made out with her, in a way.

In the late 1880s, a body was discovered drowned in the Seine in Paris. Nobody really knows what happened to her, though it's speculated that it was a suicide. More importantly, nobody knew who she was either. Unlike today, when a face might make the papers and be identified that way, in France from around 1881 they would take your corpse and hang it in a window of a chilled room, and people would gawp at your lifeless body like a sandwich in Pret. Should anyone recognise you, they would say something along the lines of 'I'll take that one to go', just like you would in Pret.

The windows were weirdly popular, in ways that were disproportionate to the number of people who were missing loved ones. 'There is not a single window in Paris that attracts more onlookers than this,' according to a volume of engravings called *Unknown Paris*.[143] Once again I ask you not to judge the people of the past, not one of whom had yet discovered *Shrek*.

Of all the people that stared at the unknown girl, not one knew who she was. She was buried in a pauper's grave, but not before one last creep took something from her: her face.

It's not known why the pathologist at the mortuary decided to make a death mask of her, though the popular story goes that he was so entranced by her beauty that he couldn't help himself,[144] which is a good indicator that he probably shouldn't work in a mortuary.

'Where's Remi gone?'

'Remi? Oh you mean the fucking creep. Yeah, he's taking another cast of a corpse he's got the hots for. I'd fire him, but he's just so goddamn good at window displays.'

For whatever reason the cast was made, it was bizarrely popular when masks reproduced from it went on sale. People could just not get enough of this dead girl's face. It was popular among artists and writers alike, and stories were written based around *L'Inconnue de la Seine*, inventing backstories for her and why she chose to drown herself. Normal. The mask became something that everybody needed to have,[145] like a Furby except with a corpse's face on it.

Her face would endure for decades. In the 1950s a toy manufacturer – Asmund S. Laerdal – whacked it onto a soft plastic doll named Anne,[146] meaning people could now squish as well as glance at her dead face. As chance would have it, Laerdal's own son had nearly drowned when he was two. When in the mid-fifties Dr Peter Safar came up with a method of resuscitation involving mouth-to-mouth and chest compressions, he went to Laerdal for help to teach it around the world. Laerdal leapt at the chance, and together they worked on a lifelike (well, ish) doll you've probably pressed your lips against at some point or

230

another if you've ever done any kind of first aid training: the Resusci Anne.

And that's why, hundreds of years after her death, she continues to get the most action of any corpse we know about.

MEN KEEP PUTTING THEIR THINGS INTO A VACUUM CLEANER

I don't know whether people just hear the word 'suck' and don't put too much thought into the logistics thereafter – or whether, having grown up watching the Teletubbies, they have a weird thing for Noo-noo – but a significant number of men have been written about in medical literature following mishaps involving sex with a vacuum cleaner.[147]

In one incident, a man claimed he was 'changing the plug of his Hoover Dustette vacuum cleaner in the nude while his wife was out shopping' when the Hoover 'turned itself on' and, wouldn't you know it, his chap became caught in there. The doctors had to reconstruct his 'meatus'. In another, a railway signalman at work in his booth leant down to pick up his tools when he 'caught his penis in a Hoover Dustette which happened to be switched on', which was incredibly bad luck. He suffered 'excessive lacerations of the glans' just from falling in there flaccid, so it's a damn good job he didn't try to have sex with the thing. One more poor man, again naked, was attempting to blow up an inflatable mattress when – would you believe it – his chap got caught up in the hose and ripped it to shreds.[148]

I know you all like to clean in the nude, but I really must stress the danger of it. One man was cleaning the stairs when he 'accidentally slipped into the end of a Hoover Dustette'. Ouch. Apparently, with a 'while I'm here' attitude, however, 'he then attempted to obtain erotic stimulation by switching the motor on and off'.

You'll note that several of the injuries were caused by the Hoover Dustette, which has a fan blade about 15cm from the tip to grind up any large particles that somehow get caught in there when your wife is out shopping. Please, everybody, stay safe out there and do the vacuuming while wearing, at the very minimum, a jock strap.

THE PEOPLE WHO WERE JAILED BECAUSE OF UNWITTING VENTRILOQUISM

In the 1960s, a method of communicating with people with communication disabilities was introduced in Denmark. The method involves a 'communication partner' – the person with the disability – who holds the arm of the 'facilitator' – a person paid to support the communication partner. The facilitator then 'assists' the communication partner by typing out the letters they want typed out on a keyboard. Despite a suspicious lack of formal education, the communication partner would prompt the facilitator to type out full sentences, and communicate with others, often for the first time. So far, so sounds a little too good to be true.

Flash forward a few decades and the practice makes its way to the US. In 1992, one facilitator – Janyce Boynton – began working with a girl called Betsy Wheaton. At first Janyce was sceptical when she was told about the method, but her hesitation soon disappeared when she worked with Betsy. She was sure that what they were typing out together on the keyboard matched up with the thoughts in Betsy's head. Betsy would ask for things, Janyce would give them to her and Betsy would look pleased. Occasionally she'd ask for sandwiches (for example) then reach for the pizza, but kids change their mind all the time, and Janyce saw this as a sign of her decision-making skills, thinking she was making independent choices. Plus it was the correct decision. Who the hell chooses sandwiches over pizza?

Then one day, Betsy became agitated and began to show an increase in violent outbursts. Anything (as Boynton later said) could have caused it: lack of sleep, illness or just a grumpy mood, or a facilitator who keeps on sitting too close. At the time, however, Janyce thought something more sinister was going on.

The messages obtained through facilitated communication began to become more worrying and dark. They would involve a lot of swear words and 'disparaging remarks about life at home'. Boynton began to suspect Betsy was the subject of abuse. The police were called, and in front of officers, the two began to spell out detailed allegations of sexual abuse perpetrated by her parents. She was immediately taken away from her family, the parents arrested and Betsy's brother interrogated to find out his role in the affair.

Then came what should have happened a long time ago: the tests. Janyce and Betsy were brought in for some blind experiments. First Janyce, and then Betsy, would be shown a picture, and neither would see what the other had seen. Then Betsy would be asked to write down what she saw. Every single time, Betsy would spell out the name of the object that Janyce had seen. Next came simple questions about Betsy's life that Janyce didn't know. Wouldn't you know it, suddenly Betsy didn't know them either. Finally, Betsy was taken outside and shown an object, held the object, and was told what the object was. By the time she got back in the room she had clearly forgotten what the object was, as she spelt out something else.

Facilitated communication, scientific research has since

indicated, is nothing more than the same automotive effect you see when you play with a ouija board. You think you aren't moving your hands, but unconsciously you very much are, hence why the glass (or in this case, a child who is under your care) moves and even spells things out. If you think a ghost is going to say something spooky about being Casper, that's what will happen. If you think you're going to find that a child prefers sandwiches, or has experienced sexual abuse, then guess what, that's going to happen too.

Janyce, to her credit, immediately became a huge proponent of stopping the voodoo shit. By describing what had happened, she first convinced another facilitator, who reacted with 'You mean all this time, I've been talking to myself?', which they had. Janyce then criticised the practice publicly, and tried to turn people against it.[149]

Facilitated learning has been thoroughly debunked now through extensive testing. When the facilitator doesn't know what the other person has seen, it never works. You essentially function like a ventriloquist (except the 'doll' has their own feelings, which you're ignoring entirely) in the belief that they can't communicate out loud but have picked up how to write and spell.

It's still used, and it wasn't even the last case of sexual abuse allegedly revealed through the method. In 2007 a family was put on trial due to accusations of sexual assault which never took place.[150] In 2011, a facilitator believed that she and the man under her care – a 31-year-old with cerebral palsy and severe cognitive disabilities – had fallen in love, through conversations they had via this method, shortly after which she was convicted of rape.[151] Like everyone else who used the method – and still uses it today – she was talking to herself.

GEOLOGICALLY GRUESOME
WAYS TO GO

There are some pretty grim ways to die, and most of them were cooked up by humans. For instance, the 'Bronze Bull' (according to legend) was a bull made of bronze (hope you're keeping up) that was hollow, and big enough for a condemned man to climb into through a little door in the side. Once he was inside, his jailers would then roast the bull. Also inside the bull, aside from a roasting man, was a series of pipes that supposedly converted the person's screams into cow moos – which, even if it was a sound so desirable that you're willing to burn someone to death for it, is a sound that is readily available from moo cows.

It was so heinous that the inventor of it was reportedly killed using the bull for being the kind of arsehole that would create such a monstrosity. It was a catch-22, a method of torture so heinous that whoever designed it was clearly a wrong 'un deserving of death by that very method.

Let's leave the man-made killing methods aside for now – because otherwise I'm just sitting here listing different ways you can take off someone's skin, which makes me feel like a psychopath – and talk a bit of the horrors the natural world has in store for you instead.

237

The missing skulls of Vesuvius

Victims of the eruption at Mount Vesuvius, 24 October, AD 79, went through some of the worst deaths imaginable. When the pyroclastic flow reached them, they were hit at 200–700°C (390–1300°F) at about 50 mph.[152] At that speed, you get about two seconds to think 'Hmm, that meat smells nice OH GOD IT'S DANIEL' about the person fifty metres from you before it cooks you alive too. The extreme heat, according to a study carried out in 2018,[153] showed signs of causing 'rapid vaporization of body fluids and soft tissues of people at death due to exposure to extreme heat'. In other words their blood and other fluids boiled inside their bodies, and their flesh vaporised shortly afterwards, turning them in a few seconds from a living breathing ye olde person into a boil-in-the-bag piece of pork.

All this sounds awful, until you remember the subtitle of this segment mentioned something about missing heads. The extreme heat inside the bodies of the people trapped in the flow turned to pressure, and, as the fluid boiled inside their heads, it eventually (by which I mean a few seconds later) caused their skulls to either crack or pop off entirely like a golf ball being smacked off a tee.[154]

Lava

We've all seen the bit in *Lord of the Rings* which implies that if you fall into lava it'll be a very quick 'Agh' followed by you being dead. Unfortunately in real life, you won't 'do a Gollum'.

'You won't just bloop down through the doom soup and perish in the heat trying to fetch that shiny gleaming treasure. Lava is really dense, way denser than even the dimmest of humans, so it might be a bit like landing on a swimming pool full of custard,' geologist and author Dr Robin Andrews explained to me, with the psychopathic glint in his eyes that geologists tend to have when they chat (usually unprompted) about this kind of thing. 'You'd sink a tiny bit but you'd essentially float and splash around at first. Sounds fun – and delicious! – except this is lava, a sort of bone-melting broth vomited up from Earth's viscera.'

For the layman: lava = hot. The second you attempt to go for a splash, bad things start to happen. 'You'd begin melting, and the water in your skin would be trying very hard to escape out your body, which is obviously not great. Your nerve endings may be destroyed quickly enough that you wouldn't feel too much pain in the limbs that had dipped into the lava, but as you're being sautéed, any of your protuberances still poking above the surface may experience a few more moments of agony.'

At this point Dr Andrews has basically got a full erection. I steer the conversation towards any comfort that can be gained for Gollum fans who don't like the image of him slowly being fried from the feet upwards. 'If you're very lucky, the thermal shock to your organs would make you pass out sharpish. If you fell in head first, your brain would boil, which sucks but you won't feel much. And the noxious gases eructed by the lava may cause you to faint early on too, so you'd bypass the experience of feeling your skin turn into a sort of leather.

'All things considered, I'd advise not falling into lava.' Wise words indeed.

THE BADASS NAZI KILLER
WHO DIDN'T GET THE
CREDIT SHE'S OWED

Mariya Vasilyevna Oktyabrskaya was one of the most badass people you've never heard of. Born on 16 August 1905 on the Crimean Peninsula, she lived a simple life in a poor family, eventually working in a factory that put beans into tins (amongst other things), where her badassery failed to shine.

In 1925, she married an officer in the Soviet army and started to take an interest in military matters. Putting her bean days well and truly behind her, she trained as an army nurse, and learnt how to fire weapons and drive various vehicles, which was unusual for the time. When World War II started, however, she was evacuated to Siberia while her husband was sent to fight. She spent a couple of years in Tomsk before she received a letter informing her that her husband had been killed in Kiev, two years before.

In a rage that was probably partly to do with the postal system – you're pissy when your Amazon package doesn't show up after a few days, imagine how livid you'd be if it arrived years late with a note that read 'boyfriend = corpse' – she sold all of her possessions and immediately wrote a letter to Stalin. 'My husband was killed in action defending the motherland,' she began. Shit is getting serious when you start referring to 'the motherland', in my experience.

'I want revenge on the fascist dogs for his death and for the death of Soviet people tortured by the fascist barbarians. For this purpose, I've deposited all my personal savings – 50,000 rubles – to the National Bank in order to build a tank. I kindly ask to name the tank "Fighting Girlfriend" and to send me to the front line as a driver of the said tank.'

Stalin and his goons went for it, thinking it could be a morale-raising stunt for the troops and population to see a widow on a bloodthirsty rampage of vengeance.[155] Of course, if she was there mainly for morale, they didn't want her to die right away. It hardly raises spirits if you say 'Check out this badass going to the front line aaaaand she's dead. Fell on her own grenade. Still, pretty inspiring bits of meat flying around though, eh? Smush them around a bit and maybe they'll read "GO SOVIETS".' She was given five months of tank training, much more than the usual 'this one goes forward, try not to become a dead' given to troops at the time.

Soon after her training finished, she was sent to fight in the Second Battle of Smolensk on 21 October 1943, trying to clear the impressive Nazi force occupying the area. The Soviets made good on their deal and painted her tank to read 'Fighting Girlfriend', which didn't go down well with her fellow troops, who saw it as a publicity stunt. To be fair, it was a publicity stunt to Stalin, but to Oktyabrskaya it was a genuine opportunity to turn Nazis into heavily cooked Nazis. They also saw it as a joke, just as Oktyabrskaya saw smattering the brains of Nazis with tank fire as a bit of a giggle, probably.

Very quickly into the battle, she showed that she knew what

she was doing, taking out machine gun nests, several artillery pieces and breaking through enemy lines all while under very heavy fire, not letting a small thing like a massively increased risk of death interrupt what was quickly becoming a rampage.[156] When her tank became damaged, she was ordered to remain inside[157] – but, probably while muttering under her breath about not wanting to die like all those millions of baked beans she'd canned, she climbed out of the tank under heavy fire and repaired it herself while her team covered her.

She then got back in the tank and carried on fighting. Despite disobeying a direct order, she was promoted to the rank of sergeant for her heroism, and given the nickname 'Mother' by her comrades as an extra 'we're still not keen on women though so let's make you feel old' fuck you.

A month later, she took part in some more combat. This time she drove her tank at night right at the enemy's fortified defences, going over dugouts and crushing machine gun nests like mashed beans, probably yelling the Russian equivalent of 'Yeeeehawww, let's take this bitch off-road'. Again, the tank was damaged – this time it was the tracks – and she disobeyed orders once more, jumping out with a comrade to fix it, all while being under heavy fire at night.

Having undertaken two Nazi-killing rampages, she had more than proved herself, to her country and to the spooky ghost she was avenging, but, unfortunately for the Nazis, she wasn't done yet. She decided the best way to round off two courses of killing sprees was with a third killing spree – a rampage pudding, if you will. Two months after her second battle, she again went full berserker and took out a bunch of Nazi defences, probably finding it all a bit vanilla by this point, maybe even thinking about getting back into beans when this was all over. Again her tank took damage, and she immediately jumped out like a badass one final time. She made the repairs, but was hit in the head by shrapnel from a nearby anti-tank shell, and knocked unconscious. A few months later, she died, and was made a Hero of the Soviet Union thereafter.

THE RICHEST MAN WHO EVER LIVED BANKRUPTED CITIES BY SIMPLY VISITING THEM

The wealthiest man who ever lived isn't one of the giants that exploits their workers, or the tech bro with glasses who is somehow such a super-genius that he's capable of a global conspiracy to microchip everybody through vaccines but can't make a search engine that isn't Bing. Though I'm glad of that, I'm reluctant to call it a huge win given that they could give away $100 billion of their money and still never be forced to buy budget sausages or drive anything less flashy than a private jet.

No, the wealthiest man who ever lived was Emperor Musa I of Mali, estimated to be worth about $400 billion.[158] It's difficult to portray how much money that is. Saying you could trade two Bezoses for him and you'd still need to throw in a Murdoch to sweeten the deal makes him sound poor – because if there were two Bezoses and a Murdoch in your house you'd do anything you could to get rid of them. If the trade didn't go well you'd probably just shoot bug spray at them and hiss till they left your bungalow, making them ultimately valueless.

Musa, inheriting a massive empire, went on to expand it, making it stretch across 3200 kilometres of resource-rich territory and trading cities. Due to the amount of gold, salt and cowry shells – used as currency at the time – he was basically unimaginably rich.

To put it in perspective, he once went on a holiday and ended up fucking up an entire economy on the way. In 1324, the sultan of the West African Mali Empire took a pilgrimage to Mecca, a journey of a thousand miles. As the richest person who has ever lived before or since, he did not pack lightly. As well as a convoy of livestock for the journey (in the same way you might pack Pringles for the car) he took 21,000 kilograms of gold, 100 elephants, 80 camels, 12,000 slaves and 60,000 other servants for the journey.

This would be like Alan Sugar saying, 'I'm just popping off to Milan, you fancy joining me, Slough?'

Musa was incredibly generous on this trip. Even his slaves wore the finest silks and gold,[159] though I imagine if he'd asked what they really wanted for a gift they'd have said 'not to be a slave, please', so let's not get too carried away with how generous he was. When the tens of thousands arrived at Cairo he began spending lavishly. Too lavishly. I know when you're in the fray of it and some guy is throwing gold bars at you to dance or play your lute, you think 'Well, this is fucking demeaning, but look at all that cash.' But when he's also giving the same ridiculous amount of cash to the person you're buying your eggs from (in this scenario you really *love* eggs), suddenly you find that your money isn't worth as much to the now ridiculously rich egg vendor. There you are, standing there covered in gold but eggless, while the theme tune from *The Twilight Zone* plays over and over again in your head.

During the spending spree, Musa managed to devalue gold so much that he caused about $1.5 billion (£1.1 billion) of economic losses, triggering untold misery and poverty because everyone just had too much fucking gold now. It's a pretty good sign of wealth when you give away so much gold that it's now just a heavy annoyance. 'No more gold please, we're so poor and shiny.'

THE CORPSE THAT HELPED
DEFEAT HITLER

During World War II, just like the scientists who got very creative when dealing with the Covid-19 pandemic, the whole world rallied to think of inventive new ways to maim the crap out of each other. Though the Americans went big and thought atom bomb and the Nazis created devastating chemical weapons, the UK had its fair share of ideas that would make you go 'Look, I get that they're the baddies, but I think we might need to cool our tits a bit here, because from the outside we're starting to look a bit Hitler-y.'

One idea, proposed in a document named the 'Trout Memo', which was distributed amongst the chiefs of wartime intelligence in September 1939, was to get a bunch of delicious-looking food tins, fill them with explosives and push them out to sea. Then, like someone in a cartoon, the enemy would spot them, rub their eyes and scoff them down before their bellies popped out and a big 'boom' flashed across the screen. OK, I tried to make that sound cartoony to hide the grim reality that they were hoping starving sailors would desperately open the tins only to be met with a tinful of having their face blasted off with TNT. A more fun example involved a fake treasure ship buried beneath the ocean, filled with commandos instead of fancy necklaces. The ideas in the Trout Memo are thought mainly to be the work of the James Bond author, Lieutenant Commander Ian Fleming – but none of them were put into practice, except one.

Operation Mincemeat was in many ways a classic disinformation campaign. You give the enemy a false message in a way that makes them think they've intercepted a real one. The British suspected that Spanish authorities were passing on information to the Germans, which helped them hit upon a plan. 'A body is obtained from one of the London hospitals (normal peacetime price £10) it is then dressed in Army, Naval or Air Force Uniform of suitable rank,' the document named Trojan Horse read.[160] Not to digress too much from the horror show, but it's a bit disconcerting that you could pop off down to a hospital and pick up a couple of corpses for £20. It continued: 'The lungs are filled with water and the documents are disposed in an inside pocket.'

The body would then be floated to a nice Spanish beach to be picked up by the authorities, and – they hoped – the message and body would be passed on to the Nazis. The only problem – apart from the many ethical issues involved with obtaining and fucking around with corpses – was that they'd need it to be a 'fresh one'.

The core team behind Operation Mincemeat – which by the way was only slightly more disrespectful to the deceased than calling it Operation Floatycorpse – were Ewen Montagu and Charles Cholmondeley. With the help of pathologist Bernard Spilsbury, they determined that they wouldn't even need to find a drowning victim, or fill the lungs with seawater: 'if a post mortem examination was made by someone who had formed the preconceived idea that the death was probably due to drowning there was little likelihood that the difference between this liquid, in lungs that had started to decompose, and sea water would be noticed.'[161]

You know your job is a bit grisly when the sentence 'decomposing lung fluid looks a bit like sea water' triggers a high-five from your colleagues. The spooks – in every sense of the word – began to construct the identity of an officer who never existed, while they waited patiently for a suitable corpse.

Glyndwr Michael, meanwhile, was blissfully unaware of his role in the plan, being, as he was, dead. He had been found in an abandoned warehouse in King's Cross one freezing winter night,[162] his death thought to be suicide from consuming rat poison. Despite being dead, his part in the war effort wasn't yet over, and you could argue he seemed keen, given all those decomposition fluids he was helpfully pumping into his lungs, but I wouldn't advise making that argument out loud. For his lung-juice enthusiasm, he was about to be promoted to the rank of major, under his new pseudonym 'William Martin' of the Royal Marines.

He was also given a new life, in the form of documents and other crap that was deposited in his new trouser pockets after they stripped him and stuck him in a uniform. He was provided with a picture of a fiancée named Pam, a few love letters and a receipt for a diamond ring,[163] creating for him the backstory of a guy who was a bit in love but still hanging on to the receipt at all times just to be on the safe side. For his ID card they attempted to photograph the corpse, but hit a snag that was plainly obvious to any idiot – that the guy in the photograph was dead, and usually ID cards require you to be alive. You've probably never been into one of those booths in train stations and been told 'No smiles, and try to look like the worms are really going to town on your gastric juices right now.' Fortunately, despite the rush, they managed to photograph a guy who looked similar enough to the body to pass.[164]

Plans for attack were also placed on the corpse, which made it look like the Allies were going to land soon in Greece, rather than what they were actually planning to do which was to invade Sicily. He was taken by submarine out to the ocean, where on 30 April 1943, he was released in his canister, to bob his way into the history books and help win a key battle for the Allies. Before he could make his final journey, they read Psalm 39 to him, which seems respectful except a few moments later they had to machine-gun the fuck out of his canister to sink it, leaving his body to float on. When this failed, explosives were used, in possibly the least dignified ending I've ever heard of.

The corpse was found by fishermen the same day as it set off. His body was taken to pathologists in Spain and his personal effects sent on to the Nazis, just as the instigators of Operation Mincemeat had hoped. They were suckered in by old corpsey, who played his final part beautifully, and Hitler ended up convincing Mussolini that they both needed to mobilise troops to Greece pronto, while the Allies took Sicily with relative ease. All thanks to a ragtag group of good guys who were fine with doing weird dress-up doll things to a corpse.

BUTT PLUGS WERE INVENTED TO CURE HEADACHES, BAD BREATH AND INSANITY

For a very long time, the finest medical minds were preoccupied with the question: 'Can this problem be solved by putting something in the bum?'

In the 1890s, when a certain Dr Young sat down and set about solving problems, from insomnia to anorexia and indigestion, he came up with a one-size-fits-all solution: taking an increasingly large series of Dr Young's Ideal Rectal Dilators and ramming them up your arsehole. 'First warm dilator in warm water; then lubricate outside of dilator with Dr Young's Piloment (or if it is not available, with vaseline) and while in a squatting position – or while lying on the side with knees drawn up – gently insert in the rectum as far as the flange or rim,' the instructions to the dilators read.[165]

They then recommend you lie yourself down, plugged in like a toaster, for at least ten minutes, or half an hour for the best results. The one-size-fits-all solution did not come in just the one size, however. Oh no, these dildos were for people with headaches who also liked a bit of a challenge. 'When ready to go to the next larger size, it is best first to use for a few minutes the same size you have been using, inserting and withdrawing it several times. This is very beneficial and should not be overlooked.' The packaging noted that the large – let's face facts here – sex toys were not to be used by anyone under the age of eight, before ruining this obviously good-sense point by adding 'without doctor supervision'.

The plugs themselves were truly intimidatingly large, and Young noted that people would often panic at the sight of them. I'd suggest this might be partly down to the fact that they'd just told a stranger they had a cough and his response was to whip out a range of dildos – but that's just my opinion. However, Young assured everybody that they'd get used to the plugs by gently working through the sizes, and might even want to buy the secret, mega-long and extra thick Dilator Number 5. To help you on your quest was Dr Young's Piloment – essentially Vaseline, but for some reason he'd laced it with drugs including belladonna, aka deadly nightshade. Think condoms, but lined with cyanide.

Some of Dr Young's claims weren't as batshit as you'd expect from a guy who thought half an hour with a butt plug was a proportionate and time-effective response to bad breath when toothpaste already existed. He wanted the dilators to be used to relieve constipation, and to be fair to him it probably is easier to go toilet when your anus resembles a stretched jumper sleeve you've accidentally rammed your head through. Then, he claimed, it could also cure diarrhoea and flatulence, which I imagine would be the case for the entire time it's up there.

After that, his claims started to make a lot less sense. He claimed that the product promoted better sleep, could help with bad tastes in the mouth, sallow skin, acne, anaemia, lassitude, insomnia, anorexia, headaches, haemorrhoids, prolapse, indigestion, nervousness, irritability and cold extremities. For good measure, he casually threw out there that it could also cure insanity.

The claims were nonsense, as would soon be alleged in court in one of the best named cases of all time: 'U.S. v. 67 Sets of Dr. Young's Rectal Dilators and 83 Packages of Dr. Young's Piloment'. Imagine reading *To Kill A Mockingbird* as a kid, growing up dreaming of being a noble lawyer fighting injustice, then finding yourself on the prosecution against sixty-seven sets of used dildos. The US Food and Drug Administration ruled that not only were the butt plugs ineffective in curing all the conditions Dr Young had said they would, but also they 'would be dangerous to health when used with the frequency and duration prescribed, recommended, or suggested in the labeling'.

Which is why these days when you tell somebody 'I've had a bad night's sleep,' people rarely respond with 'I'll go and fetch the gigantic butt plug.'

PAINLESS PARKER, THE SHIT DENTIST WHO PUT ON A SHOW

Painless Parker (born Edgar R.R. Parker in 1872) took an unusual route to becoming a dentist. Rather than studying hard and passing his exams, he opted to fail his exams and then beg the Dean of Medicine to let this one slide.[166] In a move worthy of Boris Johnson, he didn't let the fact that he was shit at dentistry stop him from practising dentistry, and moved to Canada to get yanking teeth.

In the early days of his career, Parker wanted to go legit.[167] Soliciting customers at the time was frowned upon by the dental profession, so he sat in his new and unheard-of dental practice, waiting for someone with shit teeth to stumble through the door. Six weeks in, not one toothy shit had done so, and he needed to try other methods. Immediately abandoning his principles in favour of having enough money not to die, he decided to hit the street corners and offered to prise the teeth out of passing strangers' mouths for 50 cents per yank. He guaranteed patients that they wouldn't feel any pain, and if they did he would give them five dollars back, an undeliverable promise even for a competent dentist. He had a secret medical technique up his sleeve, however, which was to give the patient copious amounts of cocaine, followed by

255

whisky, all for the low, low price of half a dollar. He would then throw the extracted teeth into a big bucket of teeth that lay next to him – a red flag on hygiene and the 'so this guy's a fucking serial killer then' front.

The service was popular, likely because of the unaffordability of dental work at the time and all the cheap cocaine.[168] Parker was basically a crack dealer who deals such good crack that you don't mind letting him use you to practise medical procedures. You knock yourself out mate, just keep that sweet cocaine flowing.

Here's where things got really weird. Having developed a taste for the money that could be gained by simply asking strangers if they'd like to have their teeth ripped out, he wanted to move onwards and upwards. He decided to turn the dental appointments he was conducting into a travelling circus. The man hired a band, contortionists and eventually *dancing girls* to travel around with him in a horse-drawn coach to drum up crowds from whom he could rip teeth. Scale these dancing girls up to today's standards and you're probably looking at the equivalent of going into a live sex show in Amsterdam and watching some middle-aged bloke performing a fairly tricky root canal.

The coach would set up, crowds would be drawn in by all the sexy dental assistants, and then Parker would ask for a volunteer from the audience to step inside to have their teeth painlessly pulled out. This first person was always a paid stooge; up he'd clamber and dutifully open his mouth so Parker could slip out a fake tooth. The audience would then be convinced that the surgery was painless and willingly climb into his horse-drawn practice. Here's where the band paid off, because the surgery was not painless at all, even with the drugs involved. Then when he'd run out of cocaine and whisky, he'd have to extract without either.

In the carriage, the patient would look up at the man (who I should probably mention had taken to wearing a necklace of teeth[169]), and Parker would start stamping on the floor – a secret signal for the band to pump up the volume to drown out the patient's screams. The next patient would head in, probably muttering about what fucking weird choices the band was making, only to discover why. Parker would pull teeth in bulk like this, before moving swiftly on to the next unsuspecting town.

Eventually, the dental association caught up with him. Surprisingly, they weren't huge fans of a man wearing a tooth necklace tricking people into dentistry with dancing women. When they tried to shut him down over his false claims of painless treatment, however, he legally changed his first name to 'Painless' and stuck his name on the side of the carriage instead. Clever. If you wonder why the cover of my next book reads 'International Bestseller and Absolute Sex God James Felton' you'll know why. By the time he died, he had set up a franchise with twenty-eight offices and was earning $3 million a year.

ACKNOWLEDGEMENTS

My thanks to everyone at Little, Brown – from design to production – for getting the book off the ground, and to Emanuel Santos for the perfect illustrations. You are, as ever, all extremely talented people. Special thanks to Emily Barrett for the chance to write about my speciality subject: horrible things nobody would ever want to read in a million years. And for her usual excellent edits and suggestions, which improve the book no end.

Thank you to my friends and colleagues who spent months sending me horrifying things they'd found, most of which were too foul and/or depraved to make the book. Sort yourselves out, you disgust me.

ENDNOTES

1. Finn J.D. John, 'The Truth about the Legendary Exploding Whale of Florence, Oregon', *Offbeat Oregon History*, 2008, <http://www.offbeatoregon.com/H001_ExplodWhale.html> [accessed 30 January 2021].
2. Martinez, 'Thar She Blows! – Up, That Is', *Los Angeles Times*, 2004, <https://www.latimes.com/archives/la-xpm-2004-nov-15-et-martinez15-story.html> [accessed 30 January 2021].
3. Larry Bacon, 'When They Blow up a Whale, They Really Blow It Up!', *Eugene Register-Guard* (Oregon, 13 November 1970), p. 36.
4. Joris Nieuwint, 'Whiskey On The Rocks – When Sweden Woke Up To Find a Russian Submarine Stuck On a Rock', War History Online, 2015, <https://www.warhistoryonline.com/war-articles/whiskey-on-the-rocks-when-sweden-woke-up-to-find-a-russian-submarine-stuck-on-a-rock.html> [accessed 1 February 2021].
5. Yekaterina Sinelschikova, 'The Strange and Stinky Mystery behind Russia-Sweden Tensions in the 1980s', 2017, <https://www.rbth.com/science-and-tech/326583-stinky-mystery-russia-sweden> [accessed 1 February 2021].
6. Tedx Talks, 'How Herring Farts Almost Led to a Diplomatic Crisis: Magnus Wahlberg at TEDxGöteborg', <https://www.youtube.com/watch?v=xQ1Jr6QqSlE&feature=emb_logo&ab_channel=TEDxTalks> [accessed 1 February 2021].

7. Natasha Umer and Will Varner, 'Horrifying Stories Of Animals Eating Their Owners', <https://www.buzzfeednews.com/article/natashaumer/cats-eat-your-face-after-you-die> [accessed 31 January 2021].

8. M.L. Rossi, 'Postmortem Injuries by Indoor Pets', *The American Journal of Forensic Medicine and Pathology*, 15.2, 105–9.

9. Sara Garcia et al., 'The Scavenging Patterns of Feral Cats on Human Remains in an Outdoor Setting', *Journal of Forensic Sciences*, 65.3 (2020), 948–52, <https://doi.org/10.1111/1556-4029.14238>.

10. 'Cesarean Section – A Brief History: Part 1', *U.S National Library of Medicine*, 2013, <https://www.nlm.nih.gov/exhibition/cesarean/part1.html> [accessed 30 January 2021].

11. Larissa Marulli, 'Chainsaws Were Originally Invented for Helping with Childbirth, Not for Cutting Wood', *Business Insider*, 2018, <https://www.businessinsider.com/chainsaws-were-originally-invented-for-helping-childbirth-not-cutting-wood-2018-6?r=US&IR=T> [accessed 4 February 2021].

12. Rachel Nuwer, 'There Are over 200 Bodies on Mount Everest, and They're Used as Landmarks', *Smithsonian Magazine*, 2012, <https://www.smithsonianmag.com/smart-news/there-are-over-200-bodies-on-mount-everest-and-theyre-used-as-landmarks-146904416/> [accessed 30 January 2021].

13. Bronach Christina Kane, *Impotence and Virginity in the Late Medieval Ecclesiastical Court of York* (Borthwick Publications, 2008).

14. Laura Bannister, 'The Hard-on on Trial', *The Paris Review*, 2016, <https://www.theparisreview.org/blog/2016/05/18/the-hard-on-on-trial/> [accessed 1 February 2021].

15. Ian Sample, 'A Scream That Can't Be Heard', *The Guardian*, 2005, <http://www.theguardian.com/lifeandstyle/2005/feb/19/weekend.iansample> [accessed 31 January 2021].

16. Thomas G. Weiser et al., 'An Estimation of the Global Volume of Surgery: A Modelling Strategy Based on Available Data', *The Lancet*, 372.9633 (2008), 139–44, <https://doi.org/10.1016/S0140-6736(08)60878-8>.

17. Douglas G.D. Russell, William J.L. Sladen and David G. Ainley, 'Dr. George Murray Levick (1876–1956): Unpublished Notes on the Sexual Habits of the Adélie Penguin', *Polar Record*, 48.4 (2012), 387–93, <https://doi.org/10.1017/S0032247412000216>, based upon Levick's detailed field observations at Cape Adare (71°18′S, 170°09′E).

18. Evans, 'MoD Catalogues Its Nuclear Blunders', *The Guardian*, 2003, <http://www.theguardian.com/environment/2003/oct/13/energy.nuclearindustry> [accessed 31 January 2021].

19. Clark Rumrill, 'Aircraft 53-1876A Has Lost A Device', *American Heritage*, <https://www.americanheritage.com/aircraft-53-1876a-has-lost-device?page=1> [accessed 31 January 2021].

20. David E. Sanger, 'U.S. Confirms It Lost an H-Bomb Off Japan in '65', *New York Times*, 9 May 1989 <https://www.nytimes.com/1989/05/09/world/us-confirms-it-lost-an-h-bomb-off-japan-in-65.html>.

21. Branko Collin, 'The Eel Riots of 1886 Ended with 26 People and 1 Eel Dead', 24 Oranges, 2016, <http://www.24oranges.nl/2016/09/11/the-eel-riots-of-1886-ended-with-26-people-and-1-eel-dead/> [accessed 3 February 2021].

22. 'Palingoproer in de Jordaan' (1886), Historiek, <https://historiek.net/palingoproer-in-de-jordaan-1886/8549/> [accessed 3 February 2021].

23. J.T. Hughes, 'Miraculous Deliverance of Anne Green: An Oxford Case of Resuscitation in the Seventeenth Century', *BMJ*, 285.6357 (1982), 1792–3, <https://doi.org/10.1136/bmj.285.6357.1792>.

24. Maddy Searle, 'Rape and Pillage in GoT Eerily Similar to a

Yorkshire Conflict', Inews.co.uk, 2017, <https://inews.co.uk/culture/television/harrying-north-yorkshires-game-thrones-real-life-83844> [accessed 31 January 2021].

25. Kathleen Thompson, *Power and Border Lordship in Medieval France: The County of the Perche, 1000–1226 /* (Woodbridge, Suffolk, UK: Royal Historical Society, 2002).

26. See, for example, www.historic-uk.com/HistoryUK/HistoryofEngland/William-The-Conqueror-Exploding-Corpse/.

27. J. Cremieux, C. Veraart and M.C. Wanet, 'Development of the Air Righting Reflex in Cats Visually Deprived since Birth', *Experimental Brain Research*, 54.3 (1984), 564–6, <https://doi.org/10.1007/BF00235481>.

28. 'Toplessness – the One Victorian Taboo That Won't Go Away', BBC News, 15 November 2014, <https://www.bbc.com/news/magazine-30052071> [accessed 31 January 2021].

29. John Harvey Kellogg, *Plain Facts for Old and Young*, <https://www.gutenberg.org/files/19924/19924-h/19924-h.htm> [accessed 31 January 2021].

30. Mark Willacy, 'Japanese Holdouts Fought for Decades after WWII', Australian Broadcasting Corporation, 2010, <https://www.abc.net.au/lateline/japanese-holdouts-fought-for-decades-after-wwii/2336096> [accessed 31 January 2021].

31. John Farley, *Bilharzia: A History of Imperial Tropical Medicine*, Cambridge History of Medicine (Cambridge and New York: Cambridge University Press, 1991).

32. 'Stubbins H. Ffirth (1784–1820)', *JAMA*, 189.4 (1964), 319–20, <https://doi.org/10.1001/jama.1964.03070040069020>.

33. J. Gladstein, 'Hunter's Chancre: Did the Surgeon Give Himself Syphilis?', *Clinical Infectious Diseases*, 41.1 (2005), 128, <https://doi.org/10.1086/430834>.

34. 'Charles Babbage', New World Encyclopedia, <https://www.

newworldencyclopedia.org/entry/Charles_Babbage> [accessed 31 January 2021].

35. K. Drasner, 'Spinal Anaesthesia: A Century of Refinement, and Failure Is Still an Option', *British Journal of Anaesthesia*, 102.6 (2009), 729–30, <https://doi.org/10.1093/bja/aep085>.

36. 'This Real-Life Whaling Disaster Inspired "Moby-Dick"', <https://www.nationalgeographic.com/history/magazine/2016/11-12/whaling-essex-sperm-whale-nantucket-moby-dick-melville/> [accessed 31 January 2021].

37. Sims, 'Teenage Girl Dies after Not Going to Toilet for Eight Weeks', *The Independent*, 2015, <https://www.independent.co.uk/life-style/health-and-families/health-news/teenage-girl-dies-heart-attack-after-not-going-toilet-eight-weeks-10357533.html> [accessed 31 January 2021].

38. 'Toilet-Strike Drug Suspect's Charges Dropped', BBC News, 7 March 2018, <https://www.bbc.com/news/uk-england-essex-43317449> [accessed 31 January 2021].

39. Joseph P. Myers, 'Escherichia Coli Pyelonephritis, Bacteremia and Septic Shock Due to Human Wine Decanting', *Infectious Diseases in Clinical Practice*, 23.6 (2015), 343, <https://doi.org/10.1097/IPC.0000000000000298>.

40. James Morrison, 'CIA's "Spy Cat" Goes Splat', *The Independent*, <https://www.independent.co.uk/news/world/americas/cia-s-spy-cat-goes-splat-9260648.html> [accessed 31 January 2021].

41. 'Eilmer The Flying Monk', Athelstan Museum, <https://www.athelstanmuseum.org.uk/malmesbury-history/people/eilmer-the-flying-monk/> [accessed 31 January 2021].

42. Eric Grundhauser, 'The Sad Tale of the "Flying Tailor"', *Atlas Obscura*, 500 <http://www.atlasobscura.com/articles/flying-tailor-eiffel-paris-france-parachute> [accessed 4 February 2021].

43. 'People On TikTok Are Dipping Their Testicles In Soy Sauce

To See If They Can Taste It', *Men's Health Magazine Australia*, <https://www.menshealth.com.au/tiktok-dipping-testicles-in-soy-sauce-taste-buds> [accessed 3 February 2021].

44. Matt Simon, 'Absurd Creature of the Week: The Parasitic Worm That Turns Crickets Into Suicidal Maniacs', *Wired*, <https://www.wired.com/2014/05/absurd-creature-horsehair-worm/> [accessed 31 January 2021].

45. Richard C. Brusca and Matthew R. Gilligan, 'Tongue Replacement in a Marine Fish (Lutjanus Guttatus) by a Parasitic Isopod (Crustacea: Isopoda)', *Copeia*, 1983.3 (1983), 813 <https://doi.org/10.2307/1444352>.

46. 'This Killer Fungus Turns Flies into Zombies', KQED, <https://www.kqed.org/science/1949314/this-killer-fungus-turns-flies-into-zombies> [accessed 31 January 2021].

47. Min Wang et al., 'Monocular Lens Dislocation due to Vomiting-a Case Report', *BMC Ophthalmology*, 18.1 (2018), <https://doi.org/10.1186/s12886-017-0651-8>.

48. Wanding Yang, Raguwinder S. Sahota and Sudip Das, 'Snap, Crackle and Pop: When Sneezing Leads to Crackling in the Neck', *BMJ Case Reports*, 2018, bcr-2016-218906, <https://doi.org/10.1136/bcr-2016-218906>.

49. 'The Curious Case of Mary Toft', <https://www.gla.ac.uk/myglasgow/library/files/special/exhibns/month/aug2009.html> [accessed 31 January 2021].

50. Natasha Ishak, 'That Time 60 Nobles Drowned In A Chamber Of Poop In 12th-Century Germany', All That's Interesting, 2020, <https://allthatsinteresting.com/erfurt-latrine-disaster> [accessed 1 February 2021].

51. Karen Abbott, 'The Man Who Wouldn't Die', *Smithsonian Magazine*, <https://www.smithsonianmag.com/history/the-man-who-wouldnt-die-89417903/> [accessed 1 February 2021].

52. Dave Anthony and Gareth Reynolds, *The United States of*

Absurdity: Untold Stories from American History (Potter/Ten Speed/Harmony/Rodale, 2017).

53. 'Michael Malloy – the Irishman That Could Not Be Murdered', 2017 <https://www.irishcentral.com/roots/history/michael-malloy-irishman-could-not-murdered> [accessed 5 February 2021].

54. 'MAGPIE ALERT! For Aussies to Share Swooping Magpie Attacks Across Australia', *Magpie Alert!* <http://www.magpiealert.com/> [accessed 1 February 2021].

55. Mark Bonta et al., 'Intentional Fire-Spreading by "Firehawk" Raptors in Northern Australia', *Journal of Ethnobiology*, 37.4 (2017), 700, <https://doi.org/10.2993/0278-0771-37.4.700>.

56. Amanda Burdon, 'Gympie Gympie: Once Stung, Never Forgotten', *Australian Geographic* <https://www.australiangeographic.com.au/topics/science-environment/2009/06/gympie-gympie-once-stung-never-forgotten/> [accessed 1 February 2021].

57. Sandee LaMotte CNN, 'The Swedish Cavity Experiments: How Dentists Rotted the Teeth of the Mentally Handicapped to Study Candy's Effect', CNN, <https://www.cnn.com/2019/10/30/health/swedish-cavity-experiment-wellness/index.html> [accessed 1 February 2021].

58. 'Sugar Experiments of Mental Patients', *Innovations Report*, 2006, <https://www.innovations-report.com/health-and-medicine/report-57360/> [accessed 1 February 2021].

59. Dylan Matthews, '36 Years Ago Today, One Man Saved Us from World-Ending Nuclear War', Vox, 2018, <https://www.vox.com/2018/9/26/17905796/nuclear-war-1983-stanislav-petrov-soviet-union> [accessed 1 February 2021].

60. Allan Little, 'How I Stopped Nuclear War', BBC News, <http://news.bbc.co.uk/1/hi/world/europe/198173.stm> [accessed 1 February 2021].

61. Kiona N. Smith, 'The Computer That Almost Started A

Nuclear War, And The Man Who Stopped It', *Forbes*, <https://www.forbes.com/sites/kionasmith/2018/09/25/the-computer-that-almost-started-a-nuclear-war-and-the-man-who-stopped-it/> [accessed 1 February 2021].

62. 'DIED OF LAUGHTER', *The Register* (Adelaide, SA), 18 October 1929, <http://nla.gov.au/nla.news-article57926179> [accessed 1 February 2021].

63. Dragos Mitrica, 'Roland Le Fartere – a Medieval Flatulist from the 12th Century', *ZME Science*, 2014, <https://www.zmescience.com/other/offbeat-other/roland-le-fartere-medieval-flatulist-12th-century/> [accessed 5 February 2021].

64. Hartzman, 'Le Petomane and His Fantastic Farts at the Moulin Rouge', *Weird Historian*, 2017, <https://www.weirdhistorian.com/le-petomane/> [accessed 1 February 2021].

65. Sam Kean, 'What Can We Learn About Farting From the World's Most Famous Flatulence Artist?', *Slate Magazine*, 2017, <https://slate.com/technology/2017/07/lessons-on-flatulence-from-a-fart-artist.html> [accessed 1 February 2021].

66. Nick Bostrom, 'Where Are They?', *MIT Technology Review*, <https://www.technologyreview.com/2008/04/22/220999/where-are-they/> [accessed 1 February 2021].

67. Andrews, '8 Unusual Facts About the 1904 St. Louis Olympics', *HISTORY*, <https://www.history.com/news/8-unusual-facts-about-the-1904-st-louis-olympics> [accessed 1 February 2021].

68. Jake Sturmer and Rebecca Armitage, 'The 1904 Olympic Marathon May Have Been the Dumbest Race Ever Run', 2020, <https://www.abc.net.au/news/2020-07-26/the-wildest-olympic-event-in-modern-history/12467362> [accessed 1 February 2021].

69. Kathryn Harkup, 'The Cocktail of Poison and Brandy That Led to Olympic Gold', *The Guardian*, 2016, <http://www.

theguardian.com/science/blog/2016/jul/21/the-cocktail-of-poison-and-brandy-that-led-to-olympic-gold-strychnine> [accessed 1 February 2021].

70. 'The Mysterious Death of George Washington', National Constitution Center, <https://constitutioncenter.org/blog/the-mysterious-death-of-george-washington> [accessed 1 February 2021].

71. Laura Dean, *Blood Transfusions and the Immune System*, National Center for Biotechnology Information (US), 2005, <https://www.ncbi.nlm.nih.gov/books/NBK2265/> [accessed 1 February 2021].

72. Kat Eschner, '350 Years Ago, A Doctor Performed the First Human Blood Transfusion. A Sheep Was Involved', *Smithsonian Magazine*, <https://www.smithsonianmag.com/smart-news/350-years-ago-doctor-performed-first-human-blood-transfusion-sheep-was-involved-180963631/> [accessed 1 February 2021].

73. Ceylan Yeginsu, '"Dog Suicide Bridge": Why Do So Many Pets Keep Leaping Into a Scottish Gorge?', *New York Times*, 2019, <https://www.nytimes.com/2019/03/27/world/europe/scotland-overtoun-bridge-dog-suicide.html>.

74. Justin Nobel, 'Do Animals Commit Suicide? A Scientific Debate', *Time*, 19 March 2010, <http://content.time.com/time/health/article/0,8599,1973486,00.html> [accessed 1 February 2021].

75. Mark McGivern, 'Police Called in to Investigate Cow Suicides in Switzerland', *Daily Record*, 2009, <http://www.dailyrecord.co.uk/news/uk-world-news/police-called-in-to-investigate-cow-suicides-1035158> [accessed 1 February 2021].

76. Ron Grossman, 'A FOOTNOTE ON ANDY THE GOOSE', *Chicago Tribune*, 1993, <https://web.archive.org/web/20190514202121/https://www.chicagotribune.com/

news/ct-xpm-1993-06-27-9306270182-story.html> [accessed 1 February 2021].

77. 'New Strategy In A War On The Emu', *The Sunday Herald*, 5 July 1953, <http://nla.gov.au/nla.news-article18516559> [accessed 2 February 2021].

78. Bec Crew, 'The Great Emu War: In Which Some Large, Flightless Birds Unwittingly Foiled the Australian Army', *Scientific American* Blog Network, 2014 <https://blogs. scientificamerican.com/running-ponies/the-great-emu-war-in-which-some-large-flightless-birds-unwittingly-foiled-the-australian-army/> [accessed 2 February 2021].

79. 'It's No Flight of Fancy: Emus Are Birdbrains', *Sydney Morning Herald*, 2005, <https://www.smh.com.au/national/its-no-flight-of-fancy-emus-are-birdbrains-20050222-gdks8m. html> [accessed 1 February 2021].

80. 'Q-Tip-Off: Police Fear "Serial Killer" Was Just DNA Contamination', *Der Spiegel*, 2009 <https://www.spiegel.de/international/germany/q-tip-off-police-fear-serial-killer-was-just-dna-contamination-a-615608.html> [accessed 2 February 2021].

81. Temko, 'Germany's Hunt for the Murderer Known as "the Woman without a Face"', *The Guardian*, 2008, <http://www. theguardian.com/lifeandstyle/2008/nov/09/germany-serial-killer> [accessed 2 February 2021].

82. J.C. Giertsen et al., 'An Explosive Decompression Accident', *The American Journal of Forensic Medicine and Pathology*, 9.2 (1988), 94–101, <https://doi.org/10.1097/00000433-198806000-00002>.

83. 'DOG A FAKE HERO, Pushes Children Into the Seine to Rescue Them and Win Beefsteaks', *New York Times*, 2 February 1908, <https://www.nytimes.com/1908/02/02/archives/dog-a-fake-hero-pushes-children-into-the-seine-to-rescue-them-and.html> [accessed 2 February 2021].

84. Carolyn Harris, 'The Murder of Rasputin, 100 Years Later', *Smithsonian Magazine* <https://www.smithsonianmag.com/history/murder-rasputin-100-years-later-180961572/> [accessed 1 February 2021].

85. Great Britain and Air Accidents Investigation Branch, *Report on the Accident to BAC One-Eleven, G-BJRT over Didcot, Oxfordshire on 10 June 1990* (London: HMSO, 1992).

86. Michael G. Vann, 'Of Rats, Rice, and Race: The Great Hanoi Rat Massacre, an Episode in French Colonial History', *French Colonial History*, 4.1 (2003), 191–203, <https://doi.org/10.1353/fch.2003.0027>.

87. Maureen O'Connor, 'World Record-Setting Kick to the Groin Raises Five Perplexing Questions', Gawker <http://gawker.com/5472603/world-record-setting-kick-to-the-groin-raises-five-perplexing-questions> [accessed 2 February 2021].

88. Bruce Y. Lee, 'Man With Condition Called "Pica" Swallowed Hundreds Of Coins And Nails', *Forbes*, 2017, <https://www.forbes.com/sites/brucelee/2017/11/28/man-swallowed-hundreds-of-coins-and-nails-what-is-pica/?sh=411bad7b50b9> [accessed 2 February 2021].

89. Steve Moramarco, '10 Stupidest World Records', Oddee, <https://www.oddee.com/item_99645.aspx> [accessed 2 February 2021].

90. Jordan Kushins, 'That Time Cleveland Released 1.5 Million Balloons and Chaos Ensued', Gizmodo, 2014, <https://gizmodo.com/that-time-cleveland-released-1-5-million-balloons-and-c-1565731191> [accessed 2 February 2021].

91. Sinead O'Carroll, 'The History of the Two-Headed Dog Experiment', TheJournal.ie, 2013 <https://www.thejournal.ie/two-headed-dogs-794157-Feb2013/> [accessed 2 February 2021].

92. Simon Matskeplishvili, 'Vladimir Petrovich Demikhov (1916–1998)', *European Heart Journal*, 38.46 (2017), 3406–10, <https://doi.org/10.1093/eurheartj/ehx697>.

93. Marc Hartzman, 'Russian Scientist Dr. Vladimir Demikhov Created Two-Headed Dogs', Weird Historian, 2017, <https://www.weirdhistorian.com/russian-scientist-two-headed-dogs/> [accessed 2 February 2021].

94. 'Head Transplants', Dichotomistic, 2015, <https://web.archive.org/web/20150228155418/http://www.dichotomistic.com/mind_readings_head_transplant.html>.

95. Jan Hoole, 'Curious Kids: How Can Chickens Run around after Their Heads Have Been Chopped Off?', The Conversation, <http://theconversation.com/curious-kids-how-can-chickens-run-around-after-their-heads-have-been-chopped-off-103701> [accessed 2 February 2021].

96. 'The Chicken That Lived for 18 Months without a Head', BBC News, 9 September 2015, <https://www.bbc.com/news/magazine-34198390> [accessed 2 February 2021].

97. Betancourt, 'The Great Boston Molasses Flood: Why the Strange Disaster Matters Today', *The Guardian*, 2019 <http://www.theguardian.com/us-news/2019/jan/13/the-great-boston-molasses-flood-why-it-matters-modern-regulation> [accessed 2 February 2021].

98. Chuck Lyons, 'A Sticky Tragedy: The Boston Molasses Disaster', *History Today*, <https://www.historytoday.com/archive/sticky-tragedy-boston-molasses-disaster> [accessed 3 February 2021].

99. Ben Johnson, 'The London Beer Flood of 1814', Historic UK <https://www.historic-uk.com/HistoryUK/HistoryofBritain/The-London-Beer-Flood-of-1814/> [accessed 3 February 2021].

100. 'FACT CHECK: Did a Man Die Demonstrating a Window's Strength?', Snopes.com, 2000, <https://www.snopes.com/fact-check/window-strength-death/> [accessed 3 February 2021].

101. Patrick Metzger, 'Toronto Urban Legends: The Leaping

Lawyer of Bay Street', *Torontoist*, 2013 <https://torontoist. com/2013/01/urban-legends-the-leaping-lawyer-of-bay-street/> [accessed 3 February 2021].

102. Milk coke is a thing. Try it, you cowards.

103. Andrew Wulf, 'Summer of "Splitnik": Remembering the American National Exhibition in Moscow', USC Center on Public Diplomacy, 2009, <https://uscpublicdiplomacy. org/blog/summer-%E2%80%9Csplitnik%E2%80%9D-remembering-american-national-exhibition-moscow> [accessed 30 January 2021].

104. 'Nostrums and Quackery', *Journal of the American Medical Association*, LVII.16 (1911), 1315, <https://doi.org/10.1001/ jama.1911.04260100141045>.

105. Miss Cellania, 'The Strange Fate of Eben Byers', 18 November 2013, Neatorama, <https://www.neatorama.com/2013/11/18/ The-Strange-Fate-of-Eben-Byers/> [accessed 3 February 2021].

106. 'The Nazi U-Boat Sunk by a Toilet Malfunction', *The Scotsman*, <https://www.scotsman.com/whats-on/arts-and-entertainment/nazi-u-boat-sunk-toilet-malfunction-1455820> [accessed 2 February 2021].

107. Elliot Carter, 'The High-Tech Toilet That Destroyed a Submarine', War Is Boring <https://warisboring.com/the-high-tech-toilet-that-destroyed-a-submarine/> [accessed 2 February 2021].

108. 'Angry Gunman, Named Noid, Arrested In Botched Domino's Robbery, Say Police', AP News, <https://apnews. com/article/28544b5002d7d32520920549e84ddb1e> [accessed 3 February 2021].

109. Albert R. Shadle, 'Copulation in the Porcupine', *The Journal of Wildlife Management*, 10.2 (1946), 159, <https://doi. org/10.2307/3796077>.

110. Alan F. Dixson, *Primate Sexuality: Comparative Studies of*

the Prosimians, Monkeys, Apes, and Humans (Oxford: Oxford University Press, 2012).

111. Clara Moskowitz, 'Why So Many Animals Evolved to Masturbate', Livescience.com, 2011 <https://www. livescience.com/12944-animals-evolved-masturbate.html> [accessed 4 February 2021].

112. Peter Caddick-Adams, 'D-Day: Why the Training Was Deadlier than the Assault', HistoryExtra, 2019, <https:// www.historyextra.com/period/second-world-war/d-day-why-the-training-was-deadlier-than-the-assault/> [accessed 3 February 2021].

113. Nigel Lewis, *Exercise Tiger: The Dramatic True Story of a Hidden Tragedy of World War II* (New York: Prentice Hall Press, 1990).

114. Mark Townsend, 'Did Allies Kill GIs in D-Day Training Horror?', *The Guardian*, 2004, <http://www.theguardian. com/uk/2004/may/16/military.usa> [accessed 3 February 2021].

115. Laura Fitzpatrick, 'Top 10 Controversial Popes', *Time*, <http://content.time.com/time/specials/packages/ article/0,28804,1981842_1981844_1981864,00.html> [accessed 3 February 2021].

116. Remy Melina, '7 Quite Unholy Pope Scandals', Livescience. com, 2010, <https://www.livescience.com/8606-7-unholy-pope-scandals.html> [accessed 3 February 2021].

117. Bill Thomas, 'Saints and Sinner: Robert Liston', *The Bulletin of the Royal College of Surgeons of England*, 94.2 (2012), 64–5, <https://doi.org/10.1308/147363512X13189526439197>.

118. Kate Dzikiewicz, 'Dr. Liston and the Surgery That Killed Three People', Storage Room No. 2, 2018, <http://www. storagetwo.com/blog/2018/12/dr-liston-and-the-surgery-that-killed-three-people> [accessed 30 January 2021].

119. 'The Calamitous 14th Century', Delanceyplace, <https://

delanceyplace.com/view-archives.php?907> [accessed 3 February 2021].

120. Démas, 'The Great Cat Massacre: French History Revealed by the Americans', *France-Amérique*, 2018, <https://france-amerique.com/en/the-great-cat-massacre-french-history-revealed-by-the-americans/> [accessed 3 February 2021].

121. S. Thorpe, 'Monkey Weapons in the Opium War', CreatingHistory.com, 2014, <http://www.creatinghistory.com/monkey-weapons-in-the-opium-war/> [accessed 3 February 2021].

122. 'FLESH DESCENDING IN A SHOWER; AN ASTOUNDING PHENOMENON IN KENTUCKY – FRESH MEAT LIKE MUTTON OR VENISON FALLING FROM A CLEAR SKY', *New York Times*, 10 March 1876, <https://www.nytimes.com/1876/03/10/archives/flesh-descending-in-a-shower-an-astounding-phenomenon-in.html> [accessed 3 February 2021].

123. Bec Crew, 'The Great Kentucky Meat Shower Mystery Unwound by Projectile Vulture Vomit', *Scientific American*, 2014, <https://blogs.scientificamerican.com/running-ponies/the-great-kentucky-meat-shower-mystery-unwound-by-projectile-vulture-vomit/> [accessed 3 February 2021].

124. L.D. Kastenbine, 'The Kentucky Meat Shower', *Louisiana Medical News*, I & II (1876).

125. Boris Egorov, 'Why Did the Soviets Use "Suicide" Dogs to Blow up Nazi Tanks?', Russia Beyond, <https://www.rbth.com/history/329005-soviets-used-suicide-dogs> [accessed 3 February 2021].

126. Will Stewart, 'The Kamikaze Canines That Blew Themselves up to Destroy Nazi Tanks: WWII Photographs Reveal Stalin's Dogs of War That Had Explosives Strapped to Them', Mail Online, https://www.dailymail.co.uk/news/article-2517413/The-kamikaze-canines-blew-destroy-

Nazi-tanks-WWII-photographs-reveal-Stalins-dogs-war-explosives-strapped-them.html [accessed 3 February 2021].

127. Kat Eschner, 'Why the Can Opener Wasn't Invented Until Almost 50 Years After the Can', *Smithsonian Magazine*, <https://www.smithsonianmag.com/smart-news/why-can-opener-wasnt-invented-until-almost-50-years-after-can-180964590/> [accessed 3 February 2021].

128. Flavius Josephus, *The History of the Destruction Of Jerusalem (Book II)*, <https://www.gutenberg.org/files/2850/2850-h/2850-h.htm> [accessed 3 February 2021].

129. Customer service in ancient Mesopotamia: https://www.newscientist.com/article/dn27063-ancient-customer-feedback-technology-lasts-millennia/.

130. 'Victorian Strangeness: The Lawyer Who Shot Himself Proving His Case', BBC News, 15 August 2014, <https://www.bbc.com/news/blogs-magazine-monitor-28805895> [accessed 3 February 2021].

131. John Kuroski, 'This Congressman Accidentally Killed Himself In The Most Comically Ironic Way Imaginable', All That's Interesting, 2018, <https://allthatsinteresting.com/clement-vallandigham> [accessed 3 February 2021].

132. https://archives.cdn.sos.ca.gov/pdf/news-vol-4-no-2.pdf; p. 7 [accessed 12 May 2021].

133. 'Prizes Given for Squirrel Killing', *Madera Tribune*, 1 June 1918, https://cdnc.ucr.edu/cgi-bin/cdnc?a=d&d=MT19180601.2.26&srpos=8&e=------191-en--20--1--txt-txIN-%252522squirrel+tails%252522----1918---1 [accessed 12 May 2021].

134. Walter P. Taylor and Joseph Grinnell, 'California Ground Squirrels. A Bulletin Dealing with Life Histories, Habits and Control of the Ground Squirrels in California', *Journal of Mammalogy*, 1.2 (1920), 97, <https://doi.org/10.2307/1373750>.

135. Tony Dunnell, 'Tsunami Stones', Atlas Obscura, <http://

www.atlasobscura.com/places/tsunami-stones> [accessed 1
February 2021].

136. Thomas A. Sebeok, 'Pandora's Box: How and Why to
Communicate 10,000 Years into the Future', <https://www.
mat.ucsb.edu/~g.legrady/academic/courses/01sp200a/students/
enricaLovaglio/pandora/Pandora.html> [accessed 1 February
2021].

137. Donato Paolo Mancini, 'How Colour-Changing Cats
Might Warn Future Humans of Radioactive Waste', *The
Guardian*, 2017, <http://www.theguardian.com/environment/
shortcuts/2017/jan/08/colour-changing-cats-warn-radioactive-
waste-nuclear-plants-distant-descendants> [accessed 1
February 2021].

138. Helen Gordon, 'How Do You Leave a Warning That Lasts as
Long as Nuclear Waste?', <https://phys.org/news/2019-09-
nuclear.html> [accessed 1 February 2021].

139. Tia Ghose, 'Man With Hole in Stomach Revolutionized
Medicine', Livescience.com, 2013, <https://www.livescience.
com/28996-hole-in-stomach-revealed-digestion.html>
[accessed 3 February 2021].

140. D.L. Wingate, 'Experiments and Observations on the Gastric
Juice and the Physiology of Digestion', *Journal of the Royal
Society of Medicine*, 83.12 (1990), 816.

141. 'William Beaumont', 2021, <https://www.encyclopedia.com/
people/medicine/medicine-biographies/william-beaumont>
[accessed 3 February 2021].

142. Price, 'Probing the Mysteries of Human Digestion', *Science
History Institute*, 2018, <https://www.sciencehistory.org/
distillations/probing-the-mysteries-of-human-digestion>
[accessed 3 February 2021].

143. Stephanie Loke and Sarah McKernon, 'The Face of CPR',
BMJ, 2020, m3899, <https://doi.org/10.1136/bmj.m3899>.

144. Grange, 'Resusci Anne and L'Inconnue: The Mona Lisa of the

Seine', BBC News, 16 October 2013, <https://www.bbc.com/news/magazine-24534069> [accessed 3 February 2021].

145. 'Is the CPR Mannequin Modeled After the Inventor's Deceased Daughter?', Snopes.com, 2005, <https://www.snopes.com/fact-check/cpr-annie/> [accessed 3 February 2021].

146. Peter Safar, 'In Memoriam, Asmund S. Laerdal', *Prehospital and Disaster Medicine*, 1.S1 (1985), xii–xiv, <https://doi.org/10.1017/S1049023X00043569>.

147. N.D. Citron and P.J. Wade, 'Penile Injuries from Vacuum Cleaners', *BMJ*, 281.6232 (1980), 26–7, <https://doi.org/10.1136/bmj.281.6232.26-a>.

148. Dr Mark Griffiths, 'Hoover Damn! A Brief Look at Sexual Injury by Vacuum Cleaners', 2014, <https://drmarkgriffiths.wordpress.com/2014/12/22/hoover-damn-a-brief-look-at-sexual-injury-by-vacuum-cleaners/> [accessed 3 February 2021].

149. Janyce Boynton, 'Facilitated Communication—what Harm It Can Do: Confessions of a Former Facilitator', *Evidence-Based Communication Assessment and Intervention*, 6.1 (2012), 3–13, <https://doi.org/10.1080/17489539.2012.674680>.

150. Sharon Hill, 'Family Awarded Damages in Facilitated Communication Farce', *JREF*, <http://web.randi.org/2/post/2014/11/family-awarded-damages-in-facilitated-communication-farce.html> [accessed 3 February 2021].

151. 'Professor Found Guilty of Raping Disabled Man Loses Conviction Appeal', Mail Online, 2015, <https://www.dailymail.co.uk/news/article-3355178/Female-professor-guilty-raping-mute-cerebral-palsy-stricken-man-loses-appeal-conviction-overturned.html> [accessed 3 February 2021].

152. 'Pyroclastic Flows Move Fast and Destroy Everything in Their Path', United States Geological Service, <https://www.usgs.gov/natural-hazards/volcano-hazards/pyroclastic-flows-move-

fast-and-destroy-everything-their-path> [accessed 3 February 2021].

153. Pierpaolo Petrone et al., 'A Hypothesis of Sudden Body Fluid Vaporization in the 79 AD Victims of Vesuvius', ed. Siân E. Halcrow, *PLOS ONE*, 13.9 (2018), e0203210, <https://doi.org/10.1371/journal.pone.0203210>.

154. Giuseppe Mastrolorenzo et al., 'Lethal Thermal Impact at Periphery of Pyroclastic Surges: Evidences at Pompeii', ed. Jörg Langowski, *PLoS ONE*, 5.6 (2010), e11127, <https://doi.org/10.1371/journal.pone.0011127>.

155. Nikola Budanovic, 'When Her Husband Was Killed by the Nazis, She Bought a Tank and Went on a Rampage on the Eastern Front', *The Vintage News*, 2018, </2018/04/03/mariya-oktyabrskaya/> [accessed 3 February 2021].

156. Henry Sakaida and Christa Hook, *Heroines of the Soviet Union 1941–45*, Elite (Oxford: Osprey, 2003).

157. Johnson, 'Mariya Oktyabrskaya: The Fighting Girlfriend', Museum Hack, 2018, <https://museumhack.com/the-fighting-girlfriend/> [accessed 3 February 2021].

158. Naima Mohamud, 'Is Mansa Musa the Richest Man Who Ever Lived?', BBC News, 10 March 2019, <https://www.bbc.com/news/world-africa-47379458> [accessed 3 February 2021].

159. Mohamud, 'Is Mansa Musa the Richest Man Who Ever Lived?'

160. Ben Macintyre, *Operation Mincemeat: The True Spy Story that Changed the Course of World War II* (London: Bloomsbury, 2010), <https://archive.org/details/operationmince0000maci/page/6/mode/2upv>.

161. Ewen Montagu, *The Man Who Never Was* (Oxford and New York: Oxford University Press, 1996).

162. Megan Lane, 'Operation Mincemeat: How a Dead Tramp Fooled Hitler', BBC News, 3 December 2010, <https://www.

bbc.com/news/magazine-11887115> [accessed 3 February 2021].

163. Macintyre, *Operation Mincemeat*, pp. 78–9.

164. Macintyre, *Operation Mincemeat*, p. 136.

165. '335. Misbranding of Dr. Young's Rectal Dilators and Dr. Young's Piloment. U.S. v. 67 Sets of Dr. Young's Rectal Dilators and 83 Packages of Dr. Young's Piloment. Default Decrees of Condemnation and Destruction', FDA Notices of Judgment Collection, 1908–1966, US National Library of Medicine, <https://fdanj.nlm.nih.gov/catalog/ddnj00335> [accessed 24 February 2021].

166. Jennifer Billock, 'A Brief History of America's Most Outrageous Dentist', *Smithsonian Magazine*, 2016, <https://www.smithsonianmag.com/travel/remember-when-pulling-teeth-was-fun-180960448/> [accessed 24 February 2021].

167. 'Painless Parker: Part Dentist, Part Showman, All American', BBC News, 10 May 2015, <https://www.bbc.com/news/magazine-31704287> [accessed 24 February 2021].

168. 'Painless Parker: New York's Most Famous Huckster Dentist', *B & D Dental Excellence*, 2014, <https://www.rocklandsmiles.com/blog/painless-parker-new-yorks-famous-huckster-dentist/> [accessed 24 February 2021].

169. Donna Austin, 'Was He Really Painless? Painless Parker', *Cupertino News*, 2014, <https://web.archive.org/web/20140304173110/http://cupertino-news.com/?p=2712>.

Out Now

'I ABSOLUTELY LOVED IT' JAMES O'BRIEN

JAMES FELTON

52+1 TIMES BRITAIN WAS A BELLEND

THE HISTORY YOU DIDN'T GET TAUGHT AT SCHOOL

NEW CHAPTER INCLUDED!

FREAK ACCIDENT HORROR

AXING

'AS HILARIOUS AS IT IS PAINFUL'
CELEBRITY TOO SCARED TO BE NAMED

TERROR

'bloodbath'

WOT

EU

FROM THE AUTHOR OF *52 TIMES BRITAIN WAS A BELLEND*

Sunburn

JAMES FELTON

ttle f******

MIGRANTS

TRUTH

THE UNOFFICIAL HISTORY OF THE SUN NEWSPAPER IN 99 HEADLINES

VICTIMS

DISGRACE

FRI

KILLED